Art and Architecture in Vienna

Unique Walks

Maximilian Just

URBAN
EXPEDITION
EUROPE

Cover and design by JUSTePublishing

Published by JUSTePublishing

Printed in the United States of America

First edition, 2025

CONTENTS

Vienna is a handsome, lively city, and pleases me exceedingly.

—Frederic Chopin

INTRODUCTION TO VIENNA

Vienna is a city that captivates the imagination. Known for its rich history, world-class music, and opulent lifestyle, it is also a treasure trove of artistic and architectural wonders. Walking through Vienna is not merely a journey through streets and squares; it is a voyage through time, a dialogue between past and present, where every corner reveals a new layer of the city's intricate identity. From the grandeur of imperial palaces to the sleek lines of modernist structures, Vienna is a living museum of artistic evolution and architectural splendor.

Art and Architecture in Vienna – Unique Walks invites you to explore this vibrant city in the most immersive way possible: on foot. This book is not just a guide, but a companion that brings Vienna's rich artistic and architectural legacy to life.

Each step you take through the city's boulevards, hidden alleys, and expansive squares will unveil a new story, a different era, or a unique artistic vision. Whether you are a seasoned traveler, a student of architecture, or someone with a passion for the arts, this guide offers a fresh perspective on Vienna that you won't find in a typical travel book.

What makes Vienna special is the way art and architecture intermingle with daily life.

The city breathes creativity; its buildings are not just historical artifacts but part of the city's living, breathing cultural landscape.

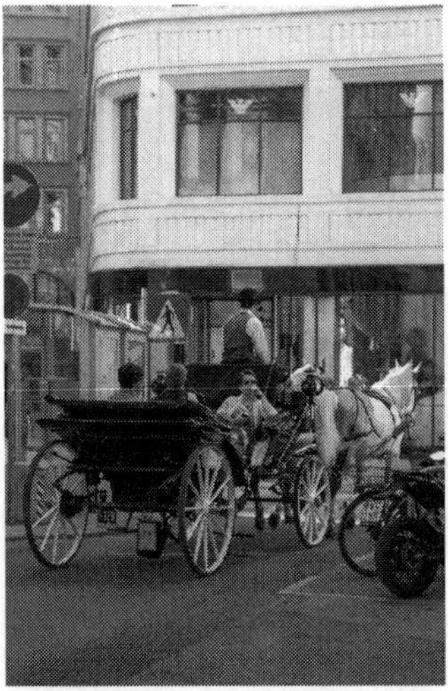

Viennese streets

In every district, you will find architecture that speaks to different epochs—from Baroque splendor to contemporary minimalism—each style telling the story of Vienna's complex history. This guide is crafted to help you engage with the city's aesthetics at every level, offering insight and interpretation along your journey.

As you flip through the pages of *Art and Architecture in Vienna – Unique Walks*, you will not only learn about the city's artistic movements and architectural styles but also how they connect to Vienna's unique cultural and historical context. This book goes beyond the surface, offering you the chance to see Vienna not just as a tourist, but as an informed observer, equipped to appreciate the nuances of its design and creative expressions.

The Architecture of Vienna: Vienna's architectural landscape is a rich tapestry woven from centuries of political, cultural, and artistic influences. The city's buildings are not just structures made of stone and mortar but are living symbols of Vienna's ever-evolving identity. The architecture of Vienna is a visual dialogue between tradition and innovation, a story told through the shapes and styles that dominate its skyline.

As you walk through Vienna, the sheer variety of architectural styles is striking. From monumental grandeur to modern minimalism, Vienna is a city that wears its history on its walls. The skyline is a dynamic reflection of the city's imperial past, political upheavals, and artistic revolutions. Vienna's architecture serves as a timeline, documenting the rise and fall of empires, the shifts in power, and the city's unwavering commitment to artistic expression. Walking through its streets is like reading a story where every building, every facade, adds a chapter.

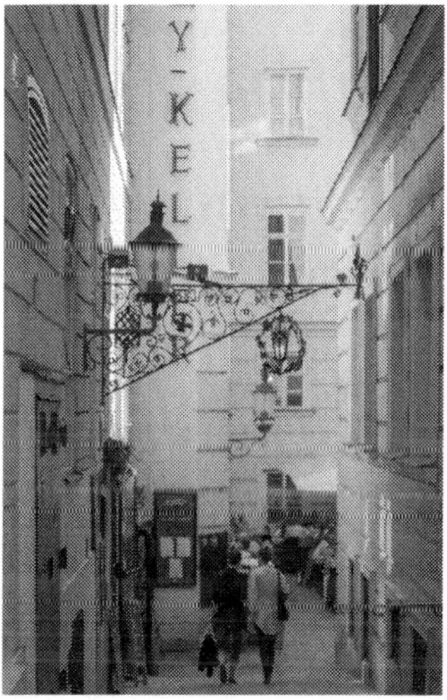

Viennese streets

The city's architecture is defined by its contrasts. The grand, ornate facades of imperial buildings stand alongside sleek, modern constructions, offering a striking juxtaposition of old and new. These contrasts do not clash but rather create a harmonious blend that speaks to Vienna's ability to adapt and evolve while honoring its past.

The city's architectural landmarks are celebrated worldwide for their beauty and significance, yet Vienna's charm also lies in the small details. The courtyards, hidden passageways, and unassuming buildings that reveal themselves to those who wander off the beaten path.

Vienna's architecture is more than a series of styles; it is a reflection of its people. Throughout the city, the influence of its rulers, architects, and visionaries is visible, from the grandiose structures that symbolize power and prestige to the more understated designs that capture the everyday life of the Viennese. Each era of Vienna's history has left its mark on the city's architectural landscape, creating a multi-layered cityscape that is both awe-inspiring and intimate.

In Vienna, architecture is not just about creating functional spaces; it's about crafting an experience. The buildings are designed to evoke emotion, to inspire reflection, and to transport those who walk by them into different periods of history.

In many ways, Vienna itself is a museum, where each corner you turn offers a new exhibit, and each building tells a story. For visitors and residents alike, Vienna's architecture is an invitation to look beyond the facade and discover the deeper narrative written into the stones of the city.

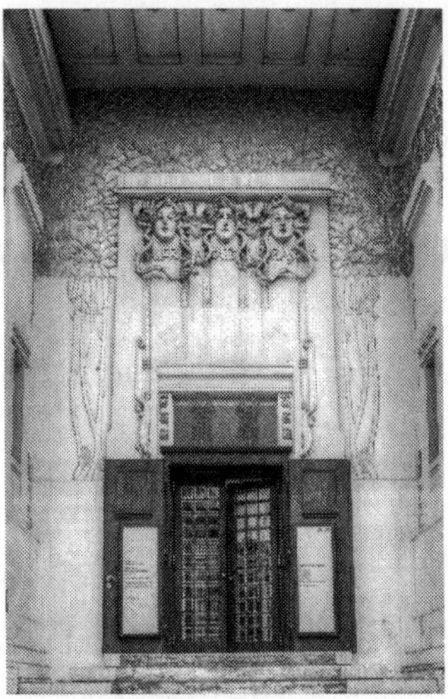

The Secession Building

The Art of Vienna: Vienna's contribution to the world of art is immeasurable, both in terms of its historical significance and its ongoing influence. For centuries, the city has been a beacon for artists, thinkers, and creators, a place where ideas could flourish and artistic movements could take root. From classical to contemporary, Vienna's artistic legacy is one of bold innovation and profound beauty.

Art in Vienna is everywhere—not just confined to the walls of galleries and museums but woven into the very fabric of the city. Public sculptures, murals, and architectural embellishments turn the city into a vast canvas. In Vienna, art is part of everyday life, whether you're admiring a mural on a quiet street or walking through a park lined with statues that pay tribute to the city's great thinkers and artists.

The city's art scene has long been defined by its embrace of the avant-garde. Vienna has a history of challenging artistic norms, pushing boundaries, and fostering radical movements. It has been a birthplace for many influential art movements, from the decorative splendor of the Baroque to the revolutionary ideas of modernism. The city was, and remains, a center for artistic experimentation, where tradition meets innovation, and where the old masters are celebrated alongside contemporary creators.

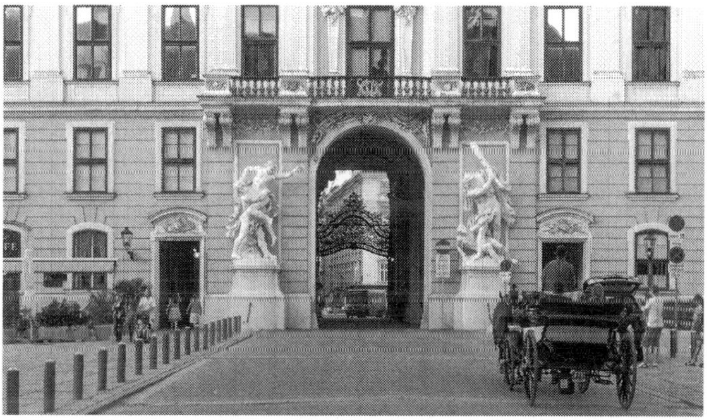

In the Hofurg Complex

Vienna's art is deeply intertwined with its cultural identity. The city's role as the capital of an empire meant that it attracted talent from across Europe, creating a vibrant, diverse art scene that reflected the broader cultural landscape of the Habsburg Empire. This cross-pollination of ideas and influences gave rise to a uniquely Viennese style—an artistic expression that is both cosmopolitan and deeply local.

What makes Vienna's art truly special is the way it engages with the viewer. It is art that demands interaction, whether through contemplation or conversation. The works of the city's artists often explore profound philosophical themes, challenging the observer to think deeply about the human condition, society, and the role of art itself. Art in Vienna is not passive; it is an active force, inviting viewers to engage, reflect, and, in many cases, rethink their perspectives.

For visitors, experiencing the art of Vienna is more than a visual journey—it's an intellectual one. The city's galleries, museums, and public spaces are filled with works that provoke thought and inspire curiosity. Whether you are a lover of classical painting, a fan of modernist movements, or simply someone who enjoys the beauty of artistic expression, Vienna offers a wealth of opportunities to explore, experience, and appreciate.

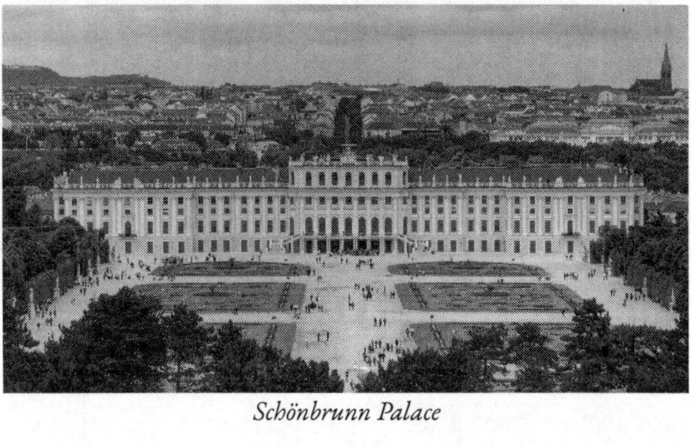

Schönbrunn Palace

Ultimately, the art of Vienna is as much about the city's future as it is about its past. As Vienna continues to evolve, so too does its art scene, constantly pushing forward, exploring new frontiers, and ensuring that Vienna remains at the heart of the global conversation about art and culture. Whether you're walking through its grand museums or discovering a hidden gallery in a quiet neighborhood, Vienna offers a rich, diverse artistic experience that will stay with you long after you've left the city. Let's now move on to the city walks we have prepared for you:

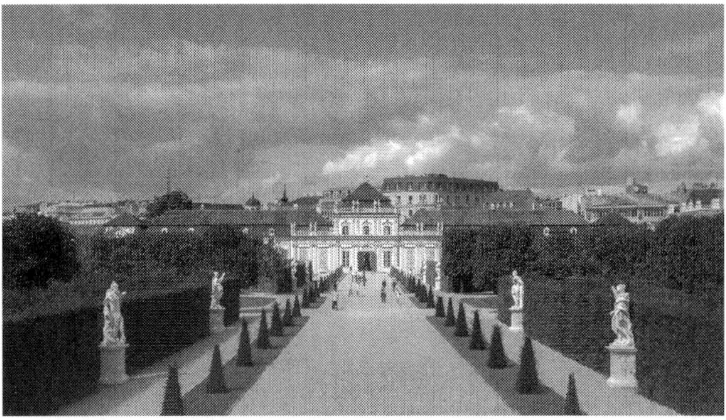

The Belvedere Palace complex

Vienna Art and Architecture Walks: Vienna is a city where every street corner offers a glimpse into its rich cultural heritage, combining imperial grandeur with avant-garde modernism. This walking tour will take you through some of the city's most iconic landmarks, focusing on art and architecture.

It is divided into **Old Town Walk – Exploring the Imperial Core** and **Old Town Walk – Art and Glory**, with details on walking distances, times, and public transport options. Along the way, you will discover fascinating historical facts and hidden gems that add to the richness of this experience.

Schönbrunn Walk: The Schönbrunn Walk takes you through the magnificent grounds of Schönbrunn Palace, once the opulent summer residence of the Habsburg dynasty. A UNESCO World Heritage site, Schönbrunn is a stunning example of Baroque architecture set amidst beautifully landscaped gardens.

This walk will guide you through the palace's grand halls, the intricacies of the Great Gallery, and up to the panoramic views of Vienna.

Along the way, explore the Schönbrunn Zoo, the Palm House, and hidden gems like the Maze. Step back in time and immerse yourself in the imperial grandeur that shaped Austrian history.

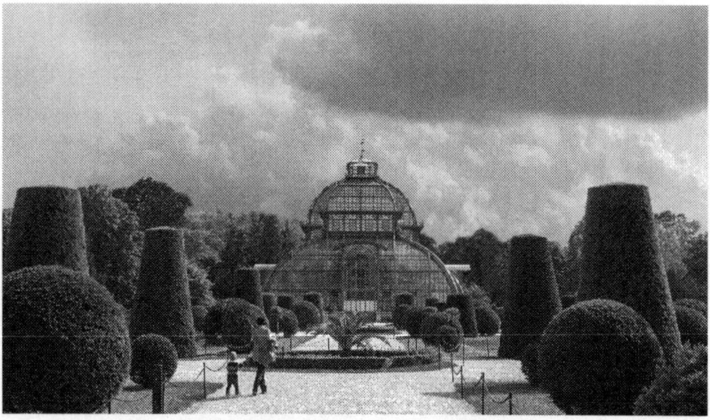

The Palm House at Schönbrunn

A Night Walk Through the Ringstrasse: The Ringstrasse, Vienna's grand boulevard, transforms into a breathtaking spectacle after dark, with its majestic buildings illuminated against the night sky. This Night Walk takes you through the heart of Vienna's architectural treasures, from the Vienna State Opera to the glowing spires of the Votive Church. As you stroll along the Ring, you'll experience the city's imperial grandeur. Discover the beauty of Neo-Renaissance, Neo-Gothic, and Baroque masterpieces as they come to life in Vienna's magical evening atmosphere.

A City for All Seasons: Vienna's charm is not limited to one season; it offers unique experiences year-round. In the spring and summer, the city comes alive with outdoor festivals, music, and long days spent wandering the streets and gardens.

Summer is particularly enchanting, as Vienna's parks and palaces become the backdrop for concerts, picnics, and leisurely boat rides along the Danube. Outdoor cafés bustle with life, and open-air cinemas and cultural events fill the warm nights.

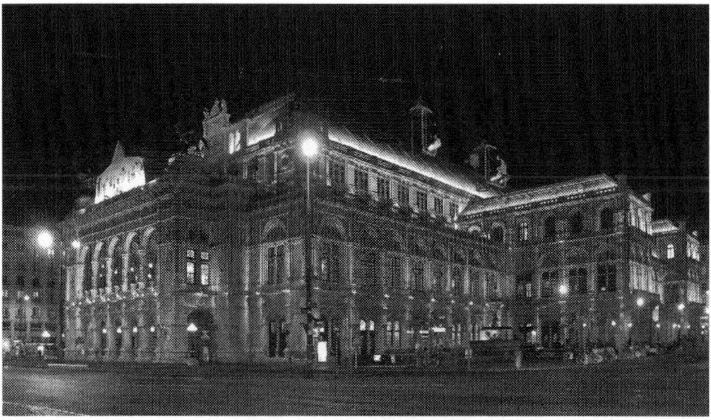

Vienna State Opera

It's the perfect time to enjoy the city's vibrant atmosphere, whether exploring its historic sights or relaxing in its lush green spaces.

In autumn, Vienna's historic streets and parks take on a golden hue, making it an ideal time to explore its architecture and museums.

Winter transforms Vienna into a magical wonderland, with its famous Christmas markets filling the city with festive lights, aromas, and cheer. The city's historic squares, adorned with twinkling lights, provide the perfect setting for a cup of mulled wine and a stroll through the snow-covered streets.

By taking these walks, you will discover Vienna's art and architecture in a way that is both personal and profound. You will move beyond the crowds and postcard-perfect views to discover the soul of the city, where art and architecture meet to create an unparalleled visual and emotional experience.

Whether you are strolling along the majestic Ringstrasse or exploring the quiet, unassuming corners of the city, this guide ensures that your walks will be filled with discovery and wonder.

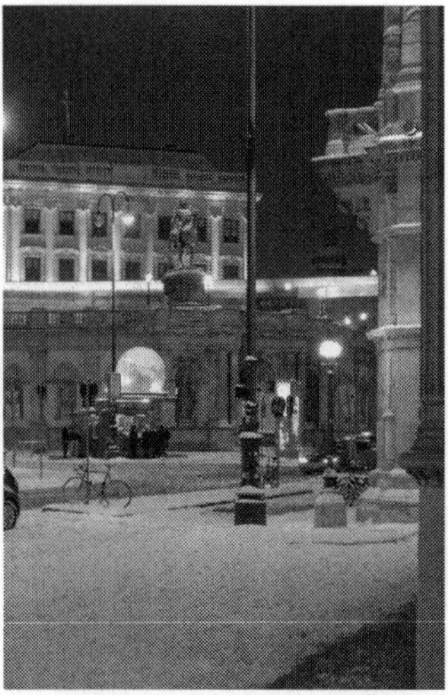
Vienna in winter

Let *Art and Architecture in Vienna – Unique Walks* be your key to unlocking Vienna's aesthetic secrets. With this book in hand, your visit to Vienna will transform into more than just a trip—it will become a journey through the very essence of art and design, imprinted on every street and structure of this extraordinary city.

Get ready to step into Vienna's world of artistic beauty, one walk at a time.

WELCOME TO VIENNA

Vienna, the capital of Austria, is a city that effortlessly blends its imperial past with vibrant modernity, making it one of Europe's most captivating destinations. Rich in history, architecture, music, and art, Vienna offers visitors a unique opportunity to experience the very heart of European culture. Once the center of the vast Habsburg Empire, the city still radiates the grandeur of its imperial legacy through its palaces, grand boulevards, and museums, while also standing as a beacon of creativity and innovation in the contemporary world.

Why is Vienna worth visiting? Because in Vienna, every step is a journey through time. The city's historic streets invite visitors to explore centuries of architectural evolution, from the Gothic spires of St. Stephen's Cathedral to the opulent Baroque palaces and the sleek modernism of the Vienna Secession. At the same time, Vienna pulses with a vibrant cultural scene, offering world-class performances, modern art exhibitions, and cutting-edge architecture. Whether you're an art lover, history enthusiast, music aficionado, or simply seeking to experience the beauty and elegance of a city rich in tradition, Vienna promises an unforgettable visit.

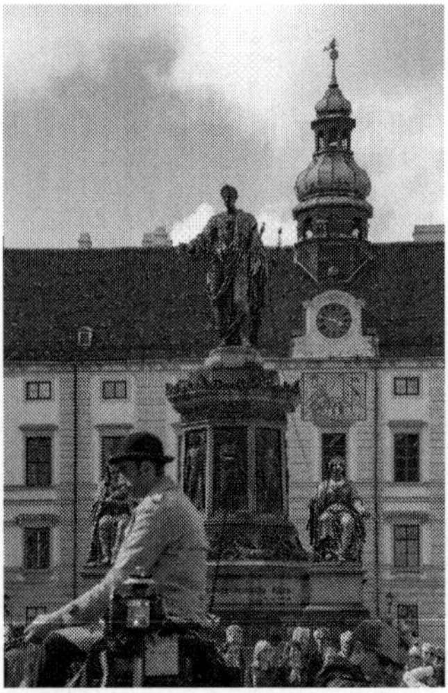
In the Hofburg

The Imperial Heart of Europe: Vienna's imperial past is one of its most defining features. As the seat of the Habsburg dynasty for centuries, it became a center of European power and influence. The grandeur of the Hofburg Palace, the summer splendor of Schönbrunn Palace, and the opulence of Belvedere Palace are physical embodiments of Vienna's royal heritage.

These grand structures not only symbolize the wealth and power of the Habsburgs but also house some of the most important cultural institutions in Europe. Inside these palaces, you can walk through rooms once inhabited by emperors, empresses, and nobles, surrounded by priceless art, extravagant furnishings, and historical artifacts that bring the city's imperial history to life.

Beyond the palaces, the Ringstrasse, a majestic boulevard circling the historic Innere Stadt, is lined with monumental buildings that echo Vienna's imperial past. The Austrian Parliament Building, Vienna City Hall, and the Burgtheater are just a few of the architectural gems that showcase Vienna's role as a center of political and cultural power.

Walking along the Ringstrasse at any time of day or night is an experience in itself, as the splendor of these structures unfolds against the backdrop of Vienna's dynamic city life.

A World Capital of Music and Art: Vienna's status as the City of Music is unparalleled. For centuries, it has been home to some of the greatest composers and musicians in history, including Wolfgang Amadeus Mozart, Ludwig van Beethoven, Johann Strauss II, and Gustav Mahler.

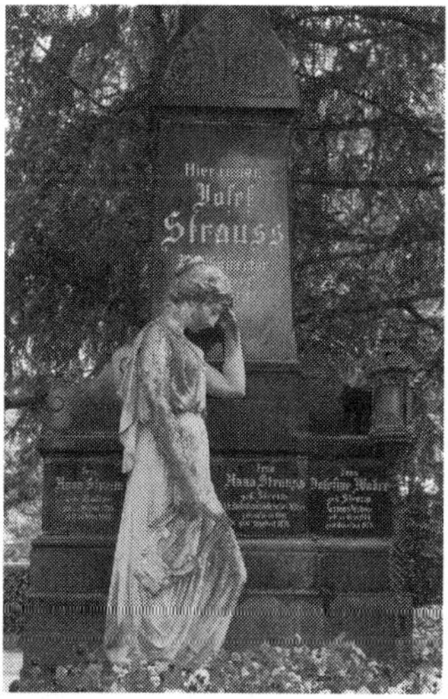

Josef Strauss (1827 - 1870)

Music is woven into the fabric of the city, and attending a performance at the Vienna State Opera, the Musikverein, or the Vienna Konzerthaus is a must for any visitor. The experience of hearing a live performance in the same halls where some of the greatest musicians have played is both humbling and awe-inspiring.

Beyond classical music, Vienna offers a rich and varied musical landscape that embraces everything from jazz and contemporary performances to experimental and modern music festivals. The city's legacy as a center of musical innovation continues to thrive, making it a destination not just for admirers of the classics but for anyone with an ear for music.

Vienna's contributions to visual art are equally remarkable. The Vienna Secession, led by Gustav Klimt in the late 19th century, was a groundbreaking movement that rejected the traditional artistic norms of the time, giving birth to modernist expression in Austria.

The iconic Secession Building, with its famous golden dome, stands as a symbol of artistic freedom and rebellion. The city's museums are filled with masterpieces by Klimt, Egon Schiele, and Oskar Kokoschka, along with a treasure trove of international art.

The Kunsthistorisches Museum, one of the largest art museums in the world, houses a vast collection of works by masters such as Bruegel, Titian, Raphael, and Caravaggio, while the Leopold Museum is home to the world's largest collection of Schiele's works.

For those interested in contemporary art, MUMOK (Museum of Modern Art) and the Albertina Museum provide dynamic exhibitions that engage with the global art scene. Whether you are drawn to Renaissance masterpieces, the expressive power of Austrian modernism, or the cutting edge of contemporary art, Vienna's cultural offerings will leave you inspired.

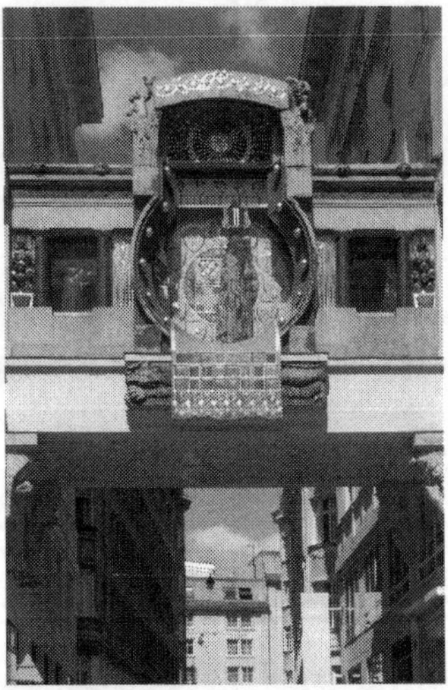

The Anker Clock by Franz Matsch (1915)

Architectural Masterpieces and Urban Beauty: Vienna's architecture is a journey through time, offering a harmonious blend of styles that span centuries. Its well-preserved historical buildings tell the story of Vienna's transformation from a medieval city to a modern capital. The Gothic grandeur of St. Stephen's Cathedral, with its intricate stonework and towering spire, is a symbol of the city's medieval history and religious importance. It stands in contrast to the Baroque masterpieces like Karlskirche, which dazzles with its dramatic dome and richly adorned interior.

The Ringstrasse, built in the mid-19th century, is a showcase of Neo-Renaissance, Neo-Gothic, and Neo-Baroque architecture, with its monumental public buildings, theaters, and museums designed to demonstrate the city's wealth and prestige. In contrast, the architectural revolution of the early 20th century, led by Otto Wagner and Adolf Loos, brought Vienna into the modern age with the development of functional, minimalist structures. Wagner's Postsparkasse and Loos' Looshaus are prime examples of how Vienna became a cradle of modernist architecture, shaping the urban landscape we see today.

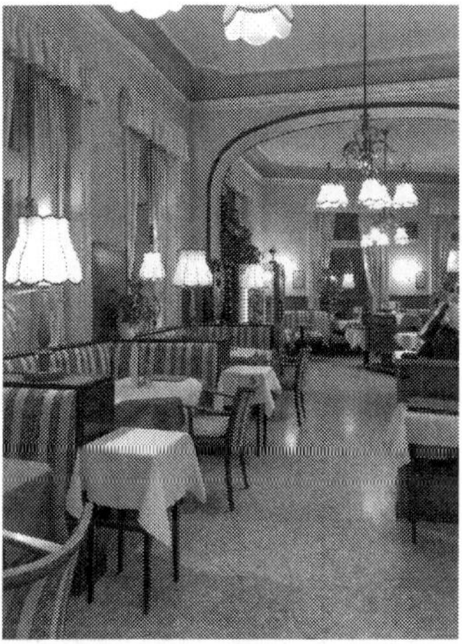
The Viennese coffee house

Café Culture: Vienna's legendary coffeehouse culture is another reason the city is worth visiting. These elegant, traditional spaces have long been a gathering place for intellectuals, artists, and writers, including Sigmund Freud, Stefan Zweig, and Arthur Schnitzler. Today, the city's cafés remain an essential part of Viennese life, offering a place to sit, relax, and enjoy a coffee while watching the world go by. Café Central, Café Sacher, and Café Demel are just a few of the historic coffeehouses where you can experience the charm and history of Vienna's café tradition.

More than just a place to enjoy a drink or a slice of Sachertorte, Vienna's cafés provide an opportunity to step into the city's intellectual and cultural history. Whether you're planning your next adventure or simply reading a book, Vienna's coffeehouses offer a tranquil and inspiring atmosphere where time seems to slow down, allowing you to soak in the ambiance of this timeless city.

Green Spaces and Palatial Gardens: Vienna is also a city of green spaces, with beautiful gardens and parks that provide an escape from the bustling urban landscape.

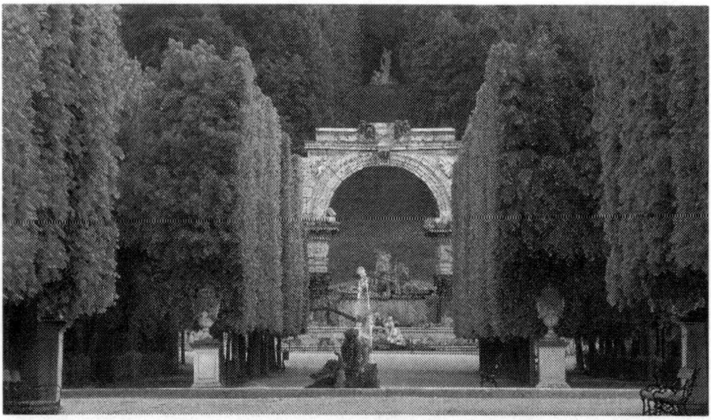

The vast gardens of Schönbrunn Palace

The vast gardens of Schönbrunn Palace and the meticulously manicured grounds of the Belvedere are perfect for peaceful strolls, while the grand Prater Park, with its iconic Giant Ferris Wheel, offers a more lively outdoor experience. The city's parks are not only places of beauty but also places where you can experience Viennese life at a slower pace, whether through a picnic, a leisurely walk, or simply sitting on a bench enjoying the view.

Imperial Grandeur: Vienna's architectural identity is deeply intertwined with its imperial past. As the seat of the Habsburg Empire, the city became a stage for grandeur, opulence, and monumental design. The Baroque era, in particular, left an indelible mark on Vienna's cityscape, most notably in its palaces, churches, and gardens.

Take Schönbrunn Palace, for example, one of the finest examples of Baroque architecture in Europe. Designed by Johann Bernhard Fischer von Erlach, this grand summer residence for the Habsburgs rivals the opulence of France's Versailles. Its sweeping gardens, elaborate state rooms, and stunning architectural symmetry reflect the power and wealth of the empire during its height. The palace serves as a testament to the cultural and artistic ambition of the Habsburgs, who sought to make Vienna the epicenter of European aristocracy.

Similarly, the Belvedere Palace, another Baroque masterpiece designed by Johann Lukas von Hildebrandt, was built as a summer residence for Prince Eugene of Savoy. It now houses one of the most important art collections in Austria, including Gustav Klimt's masterpiece, The Kiss. The Belvedere's architecture, with its lush gardens and opulent design, showcases the extravagant tastes of Vienna's aristocracy during the 18th century.

The Baroque influence is not limited to palaces. Vienna's many churches, such as St. Charles's Church (Karlskirche), designed by Fischer von Erlach, display the dramatic, ornate style that defined this period. With its iconic dome and grand façade, Karlskirche embodies the grandeur of Baroque religious architecture, where art, faith, and imperial power intersect.

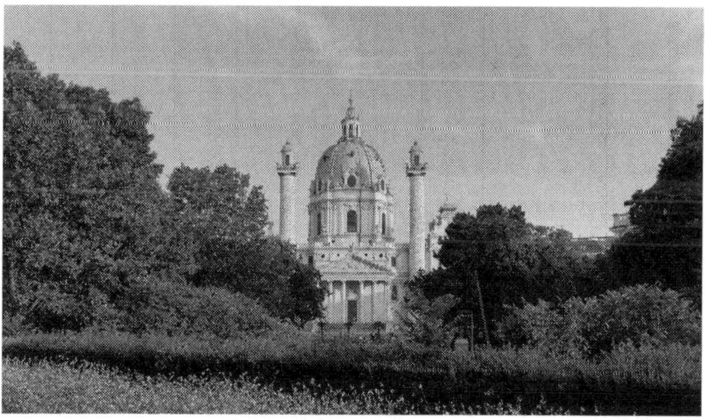

St. Charles's Church (Karlskirche)

The Vienna Secession: While Vienna is celebrated for its imperial architecture, it also played a pivotal role in the birth of modernism in the late 19th and early 20th centuries. This was a time of immense cultural transformation, led by visionaries who sought to break free from traditional artistic and architectural conventions. At the forefront of this revolution was the Vienna Secession, a movement that rejected the historicism of the past and embraced new, innovative forms of expression.

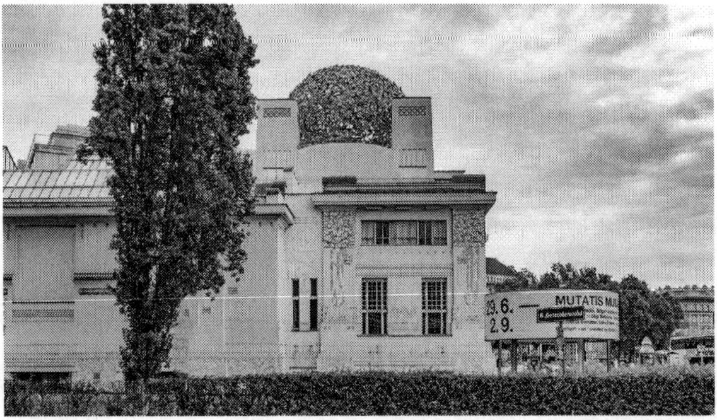

The Secession Building

The Secession Building, designed by Joseph Maria Olbrich, stands as a symbol of this artistic rebellion. With its clean lines, bold geometric patterns, and its striking golden dome adorned with laurel leaves, the Secession Building was a radical departure from the more ornate designs of the time. It became the home of artists like Gustav Klimt, Koloman Moser, and Egon Schiele, who sought to challenge traditional ideas about art and design, emphasizing freedom of expression and the synthesis of the arts.

The Secession artists were deeply influenced by Symbolism, and their works often explored themes of mysticism, eroticism, and psychological depth. Gustav Klimt's "The Beethoven Frieze," located within the Secession Building, is one of the movement's defining works, merging visual art, music, and philosophy in a way that was groundbreaking for its time. The Secession movement's influence extended beyond painting, encompassing architecture, design, and decorative arts, and it laid the foundation for modernist movements across Europe.

The Wiener Werkstätte, founded by Josef Hoffmann and Koloman Moser, further expanded on the ideals of the Secession by integrating art into everyday life. Their designs for furniture, textiles, and household objects exemplified the belief that art should permeate every aspect of human existence. The Wiener Werkstätte marked a transition from individual artistic expression to holistic design, influencing everything from interior design to fashion.

Modernism and the Rise of Functionalism: Vienna's contribution to modernist architecture is exemplified by the work of Otto Wagner, one of the most influential architects of the early 20th century. Wagner's designs embodied the shift towards functionalism and a rejection of excessive ornamentation. His work was characterized by clean lines, innovative use of materials like steel and glass, and a focus on the practical needs of urban life.

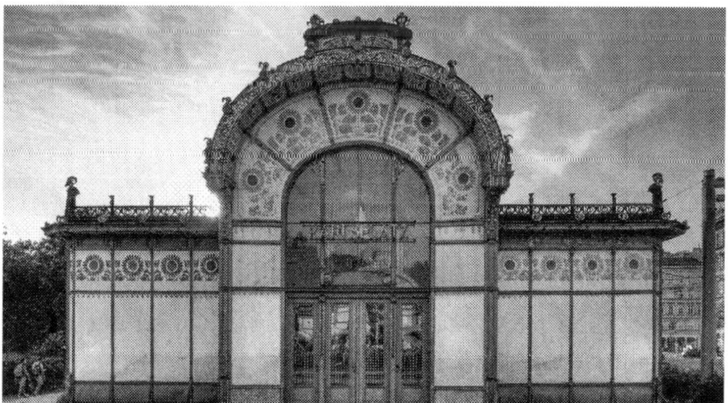

Vienna Stadtbahn railway station by Otto Wagner

Wagner's most famous projects, including the Postsparkasse (Postal Savings Bank) and his designs for the Vienna Stadtbahn railway stations, transformed Vienna's urban landscape. The Postal Savings

Bank, with its minimalist façade and functional interior, was a radical departure from the ornate designs of the previous century and became a symbol of modern efficiency and progress.

Another architect who left a lasting impact on Vienna's architectural identity was Adolf Loos, whose essay "Ornament and Crime" argued against decorative excess in architecture. Loos believed that architectural design should focus on function and simplicity, a philosophy that can be seen in his Looshaus, a stark, unadorned building that stood in direct contrast to the more decorative buildings of the time. Loos' ideas were highly influential in the development of modernist architecture, and his legacy can still be seen in contemporary Viennese design.

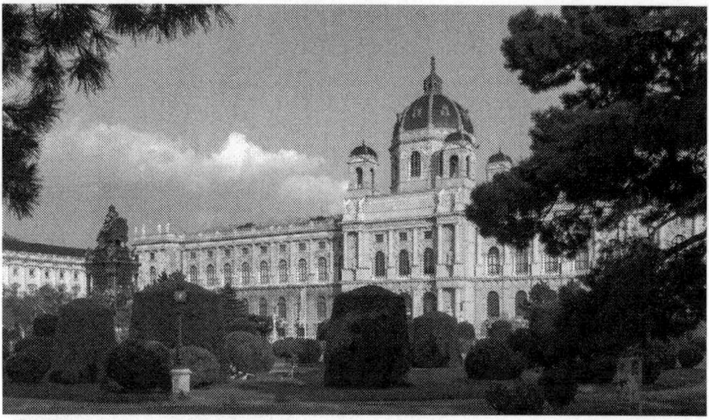

The Kunsthistorisches Museum Wien (Vienna Museum of Art History)

Vienna's Museums: Beyond its architecture, Vienna is home to some of the world's greatest museums, where art and history come together in spectacular fashion. The Kunsthistorisches Museum, with its vast collection of fine art, offers visitors a chance to see masterpieces by artists such as Titian, Velázquez, Rubens, and Bruegel. The museum itself, designed by Gottfried Semper and Karl von Hasenauer, is a stunning example of Neo-Renaissance architecture, with its grand domed structure and ornate interiors.

On the other side of the Maria-Theresien-Platz, the Naturhistorisches Museum mirrors the Kunsthistorisches in architectural design, housing an extensive collection of natural history exhibits. These twin museums are symbolic of Vienna's cultural and intellectual prowess, serving as centers of knowledge and beauty.

Meanwhile, the Leopold Museum, located in the MuseumsQuartier, is dedicated to modern Austrian art, particularly the works of Egon Schiele and Gustav Klimt.

The MuseumsQuartier itself is a fascinating blend of historic and contemporary architecture, housing institutions like MUMOK (Museum of Modern Art) and the Architekturzentrum Wien, where visitors can explore everything from contemporary art to modern architecture.

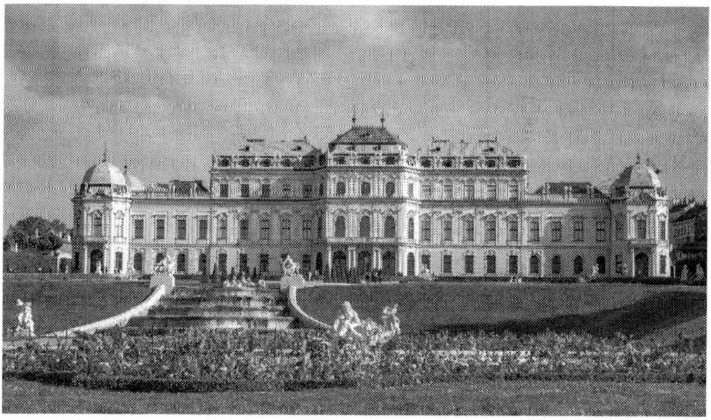

Upper Belvedere Palace

Public Transport Options: Vienna has an efficient public transportation system that includes the U-Bahn (subway), trams, and buses. For ease, consider getting a 24-hour Vienna travel pass, which allows unlimited travel on all public transport. The U-Bahn is the fastest way to travel between major sites, while trams offer scenic routes along the Ringstrasse and other picturesque parts of the city.

U-Bahn lines: U1, U2, U3, U4 are the most relevant for this tour.

Tram lines: The D and 1 lines travel along the Ringstrasse, stopping at key landmarks like the Hofburg Palace and the Kunsthistorisches Museum.

Vienna is a city that demands to be explored on foot. Its walkable layout allows you to drift effortlessly from one architectural marvel to the next, with the city's charm unfolding before you.

Our guide is carefully crafted to take you through curated routes, each meticulously designed to showcase not only the most famous landmarks like the Belvedere Palace, Hofburg, or the Vienna State Opera, but also lesser-known gems like the charming Spittelberg quarter or the avant-garde brilliance of the Secession Building.

Whether you're marveling at the grandeur of Schönbrunn Palace or discovering the intricate beauty of Vienna's hidden courtyards, this book ensures you miss nothing.

OLD TOWN WALK – EXPLORING THE IMPERIAL CORE

Stephansdom | St. Stephen's Cathedral

Address: Stephansplatz 3, 1010 Vienna

Public transport: U1, U3 to Stephansplatz

Opening hours: Mon-Sat: 6 a.m. – 10 p.m.; Sun: 7 a.m. – 10 p.m.

Online: www.stephansdom.at

Start your day in the very heart of Vienna at St. Stephen's Cathedral, the city's most recognizable Gothic landmark. Its towering south tower, at 136 meters (445 feet), offers panoramic views of Vienna if you're up for the climb.

Marvel at the cathedral's intricate spires, its colorful tiled roof, and the interior treasures such as the Gothic altar and Renaissance pulpit.

Curiosity: Beneath the cathedral is a network of catacombs where the remains of thousands of plague victims are stored. You can also see the tomb of Emperor Frederick III, an impressive Gothic sarcophagus.

Located in the heart of Vienna, St. Stephen's Cathedral (Stephansdom) is the city's most iconic Gothic structure and one of the most important landmarks in Austria.

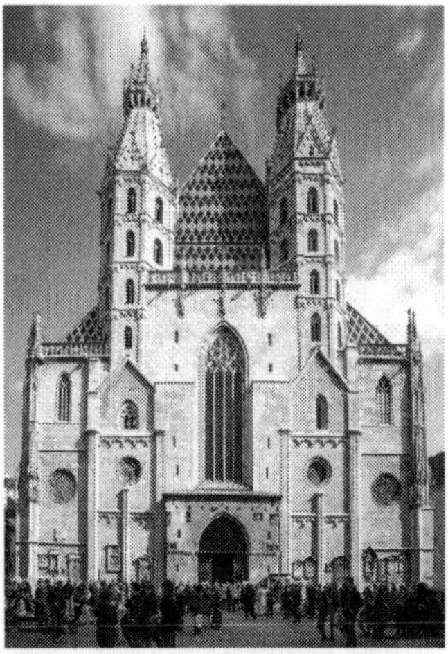
St. Stephen's Cathedral

The cathedral, with its towering spires, colorful tiled roof, and rich history, symbolizes Vienna's religious, architectural, and cultural heritage. For centuries, it has been the spiritual center of Vienna, hosting coronations, weddings, funerals, and major historical events.

A visit to St. Stephen's is a journey through Vienna's medieval past and a tribute to the architectural brilliance of the Gothic era. The cathedral's interior is equally impressive, with intricate altars, chapels, tombs, and religious artworks that reveal the deep connection between art and faith in Vienna's history.

We will explore the architectural significance and historical importance of St. Stephen's Cathedral, and provide a detailed guide on what to see during your visit, including the surrounding areas of Stephansplatz, where modern life and medieval history come together in one of the city's most vibrant districts.

Historical Overview: The history of St. Stephen's Cathedral dates back to the early 12th century, when construction of the original Romanesque church began. This first church was consecrated in 1147 and served as the foundation for the much larger Gothic cathedral that was built over several centuries. The cathedral, as we know it today, is the result of numerous expansions and reconstructions, which transformed the original Romanesque structure into a grand Gothic masterpiece.

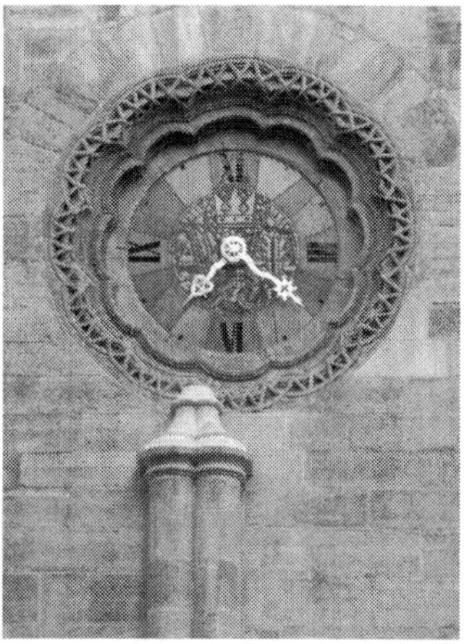

Front facade detail (manhood).

Duke Rudolf IV, known as "Rudolf the Founder," played a crucial role in shaping the cathedral's Gothic form in the 14th century. Under his direction, the south tower (Südturm) was constructed, and the nave was extended, setting the stage for the cathedral's transformation into one of the tallest and most impressive structures in Europe at the time.

Over the years, St. Stephen's became a symbol of Vienna's growing importance as a political and cultural center within the Holy Roman Empire. The cathedral has also survived significant challenges throughout its history, including fires, Ottoman sieges, and bombing during World War II.

Despite the devastation of the war, which destroyed parts of the roof and interior, St. Stephen's was rebuilt and restored, reaffirming its status as the heart of Vienna.

Architectural Highlights: The architecture of St. Stephen's Cathedral is a breathtaking example of Gothic design, with elements of Romanesque and Baroque styles reflecting the building's long history and continuous evolution. The cathedral's exterior and interior are filled with intricate details that speak to the artistry of the craftsmen who worked on the structure over the centuries.

Key architectural features:

The South Tower (Südturm): Standing at 136 meters (445 feet), this is the tallest part of the cathedral and offers panoramic views of the city for those who climb the 343 steps to the observation deck.

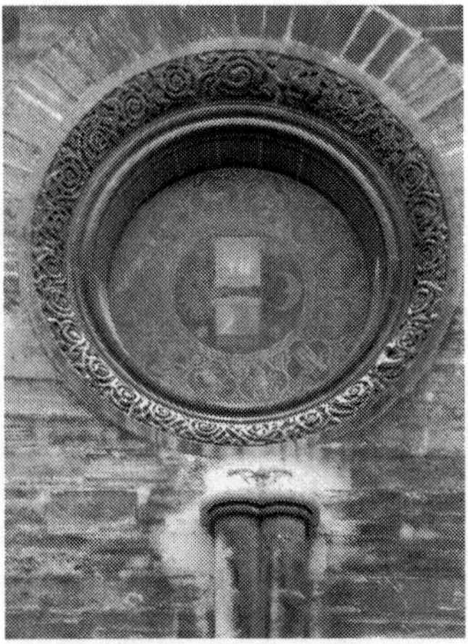
Front facade detail (lady part).

The tower was originally intended to have a twin on the north side, but the north tower was never completed and remains significantly shorter.

The Roof: St. Stephen's roof is one of its most striking features, adorned with over 230,000 glazed tiles in a vibrant pattern that depicts the double-headed eagle of the Habsburg dynasty and the coat of arms of Vienna.

The colorful roof contrasts beautifully with the Gothic stonework of the cathedral.

The North Tower (Adlerturm): The unfinished north tower is home to the Pummerin, a massive bell that was recast from cannons taken during the Second Ottoman Siege of Vienna in 1683. The Pummerin bell is one of the largest in Europe and is rung on special occasions, such as New Year's Eve.

The Main Portal (Riesentor): The Gothic main entrance, known as the "Giant's Door," features intricate stone carvings and is flanked by two Romanesque towers. The name "Giant's Door" comes from a massive mastodon bone that was found during the construction and displayed above the portal.

Inside St. Stephen's Cathedral: A Step-by-Step Guide

St. Stephen's Cathedral is filled with treasures, both artistic and religious, that make it one of the most visited sites in Vienna. Here's a suggested itinerary for exploring the key highlights of the cathedral, providing a deeper understanding of its significance.

The Nave

Estimated time: 30 minutes

Upon entering St. Stephen's, you will immediately notice the grandeur of the **nave**, which is lined with tall, slender columns that rise to support the cathedral's vaulted ceiling.

The Gothic architecture of the nave, with its ribbed vaulting and pointed arches, creates an awe-inspiring sense of verticality, drawing your eyes upwards towards the heavens.

Along the nave, you will find several significant works of religious art:

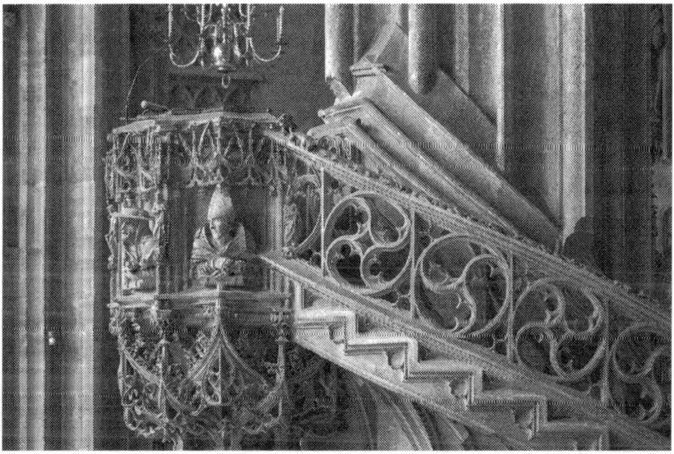

The Pulpit of St. Stephen's

The Pulpit of St. Stephen's: Designed by the Gothic sculptor Anton Pilgram, this intricately carved stone pulpit is one of the highlights of the interior. It features representations of the four Evangelists (Matthew, Mark, Luke, and John), as well as a self-portrait of Pilgram himself peeking out from beneath the pulpit stairs.

The High Altar: The Baroque high altar, dating from the 17th century, is located at the east end of the nave. It depicts the stoning of St. Stephen, the cathedral's patron saint, in a dramatic and highly detailed composition.

Curiosity: The pulpit includes a tiny, hidden window known as the Fenstergucker, a depiction of the artist himself looking out at the congregation from the base of the pulpit staircase.

The Catacombs

Estimated time: 30-40 minutes

Beneath the cathedral lies the eerie and fascinating catacombs, which can be accessed via a guided tour. The catacombs house the remains of thousands of Viennese citizens, as well as members of the clergy. The Habsburg emperors, while not buried here, have their viscera preserved in silver urns located in the catacombs as part of the imperial burial tradition.

Curiosity: The catacombs contain the remains of over 11,000 people, many of whom were victims of the Great Plague in the 18th century. Some sections of the catacombs were used to store bones in communal ossuaries.

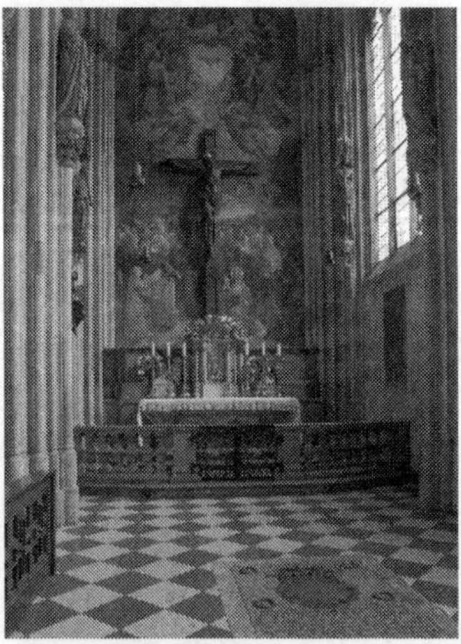
The Prinz Eugen Chapel

The Prinz Eugen Chapel

Estimated time: 10 minutes

The Prinz Eugen Chapel is a must-see, offering a glimpse into the life and legacy of one of Austria's most important historical figures: Prince Eugene of Savoy. Prince Eugene was a brilliant military commander who played a key role in defending Europe from the Ottoman Empire in the 17th and 18th centuries. His victories helped secure Austria's position as a dominant force in the region, and he became a beloved national hero. The chapel is a tribute to his legacy, adorned with Baroque sculptures and art, blending Austria's rich heritage of military, religious, and cultural importance.

Beyond his military achievements, Prince Eugene is also remembered for his patronage of the arts and architecture, with the stunning Belvedere Palace serving as a testament to his influence. Located a short distance from the Stephansdom, Belvedere Palace was his summer residence and is now a UNESCO World Heritage site, housing a world-class art collection.

South Tower Climb

Estimated time: 45 minutes

If you have the energy, climbing the South Tower is one of the most rewarding experiences at St. Stephen's Cathedral. The tower's spiral staircase leads to an observation deck with breathtaking panoramic views of Vienna.

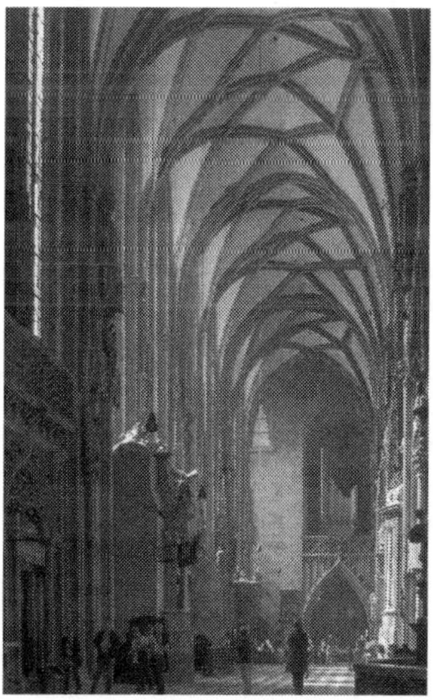

St. Stephen's Cathedral

From the top, you can see the Danube River, the rooftops of the Innere Stadt, and many of Vienna's most famous landmarks.

Curiosity: The South Tower was originally intended to have a twin, but construction of the North Tower was halted in the 16th century. The shorter North Tower was later capped with a Renaissance-style cupola.

The Treasury

Estimated time: 30 minutes

Finish your visit by exploring the cathedral treasury, which contains a rich collection of liturgical objects, including golden chalices, intricate vestments, and religious relics. Many of the items in the treasury were donated by the Habsburg emperors and reflect the wealth and piety of the imperial family.

Curiosity: The Dom Museum Wien, located near St. Stephen's Cathedral, houses one of the most significant historical artifacts in European art: the oldest known portrait of a Western ruler, Habsburg Duke Rudolf IV, from the 14th century. This remarkable portrait is a groundbreaking example of individual representation in Western art, capturing Rudolf IV's likeness with unprecedented realism for its time.

Beyond the portrait, the museum offers a rich collection of medieval and modern religious art.

Dom Museum Wien | Treasury of St. Stephen's Cathedral

Address: Stephansplatz 3, 1010 Vienna, Austria

Public transport: U-Bahn lines U1 and U3, Stephansplatz Station

Opening hours: Monday – Saturday: 10 a.m. – 12 p.m.; 1 p.m. – 4 p.m.; closed on Sundays

Online: https://dommuseum.at/tickets_en

Exploring the Surrounding Area

Once you've explored St. Stephen's Cathedral, take some time to enjoy the surrounding area of Stephansplatz, one of the most vibrant districts in Vienna. The square around the cathedral is a bustling hub of activity, with a mix of historical landmarks, modern shops, cafés, and cultural attractions.

The Haas Haus

Directly across from St. Stephen's is the modern Haas Haus, a striking postmodern building designed by architect Hans Hollein in the 1990s.

Curiosity: The Haas Haus offers one of the best views of St. Stephen's, with its reflective surfaces creating a mirrored image of the cathedral.

The Plague Column (Pestsäule)

A short walk from Stephansplatz is the Plague Column, one of the city's most famous Baroque monuments. Erected in 1679, the column commemorates the city's deliverance from the Great Plague and is an intricate work of sculpture that depicts angels, saints, and allegorical figures.

Curiosity: The column was commissioned by Emperor Leopold I, who vowed to build the monument if the plague ended. It's a fascinating example of the religious and political symbolism of the time.

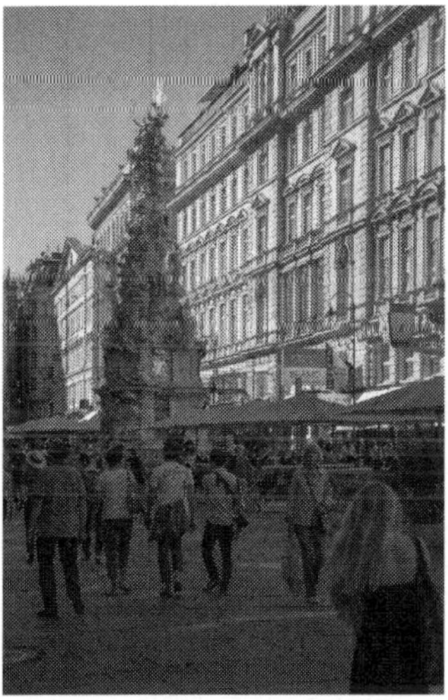

The Plague Column on Graben.

Graben and Kohlmarkt

From Stephansplatz, you can stroll along the Graben, one of Vienna's most famous shopping streets, lined with luxury boutiques, cafés, and historic buildings.

Continue to the Kohlmarkt, where you'll find the elegant Demel Café, known for its Viennese pastries and connection to the imperial court.

Curiosity: The Graben was once a defensive trench around the Roman city of Vindobona. Today, it's one of Vienna's most fashionable streets, with a mix of Baroque and modern architecture.

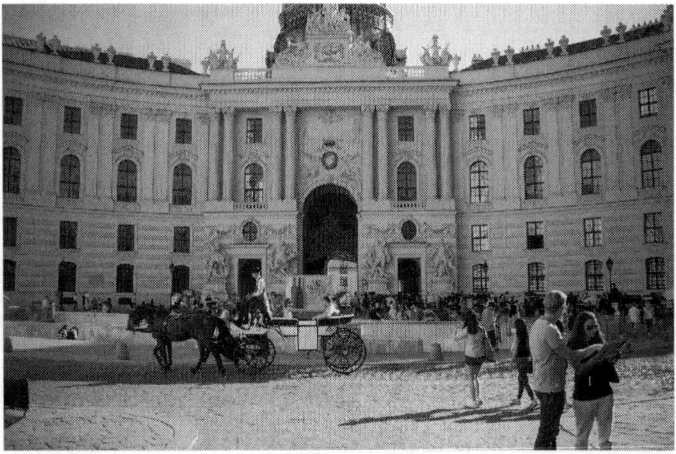

The Hofburg Palace

The Hofburg Palace

Location: Michaelerplatz 1, 1010 Vienna

Public transport: U3 to Herrengasse

Walking distance from St. Stephen's Cathedral: 850 meters / 0.53 miles

Walking time: 10-12 minutes

The Hofburg Palace served as the imperial residence of the Habsburg dynasty for over 600 years. Today, it houses various museums and official residences, including the Sisi Museum, the Imperial Apartments, and the Austrian National Library. The architecture of the Hofburg spans from Gothic to Baroque and Rococo, illustrating the evolution of styles that shaped imperial Vienna.

Curiosity: Visit the Michaelerplatz excavation nearby, where you can see the remains of a Roman settlement beneath the modern square.

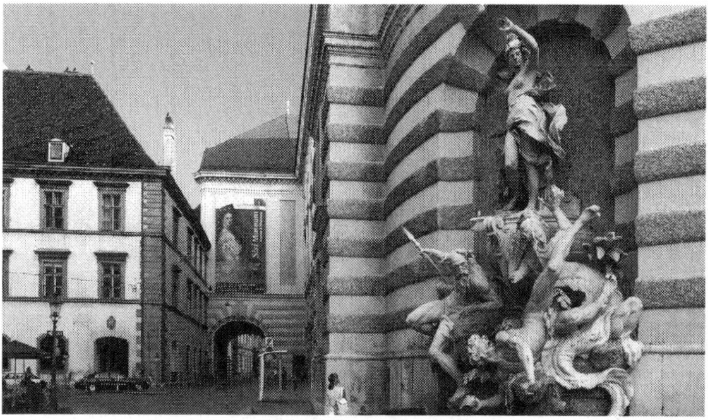

The Hofburg Palace

The Hofburg Palace is one of Vienna's most iconic and historically significant landmarks, a symbol of imperial power that has stood at the heart of the city for over 700 years. Originally built as a medieval fortress, the Hofburg evolved into a sprawling complex that served as the residence and political hub for the Habsburg dynasty, rulers of the Holy Roman Empire and later the Austro-Hungarian Empire. Today, the palace remains a symbol of Vienna's imperial grandeur and houses several museums, the Austrian president's offices, and cultural institutions. It is a living monument to Austria's royal history, filled with treasures that span centuries of art, culture, and politics.

Visiting the Hofburg Palace offers a unique opportunity to explore the multifaceted history of Vienna and its rulers. From the opulent Imperial Apartments to the rich collections of the Kunsthistorisches Museum and the Sisi Museum, the Hofburg is a must-see destination for anyone interested in European history, art, and architecture. We will delve into the history of the Hofburg Palace, explore its architectural evolution, and guide you through its many highlights, offering insights into what to see and in which order for a truly immersive experience.

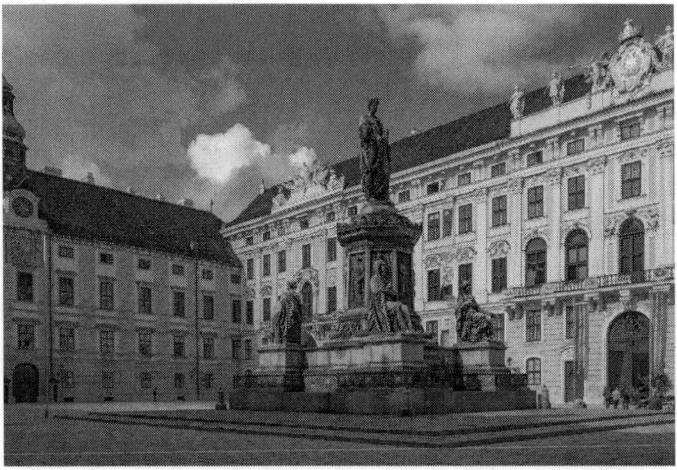

The Inner Courtyard of the Hofburg.

Historical Overview: The Hofburg Palace began as a modest medieval fortress in the 13th century, constructed by the Babenberg family, the ruling dynasty before the Habsburgs. It was later expanded by Rudolf I of Habsburg, who made the Hofburg the center of his rule after becoming King of the Romans in 1273. Over the centuries, each generation of Habsburg rulers contributed to the expansion of the Hofburg, resulting in the sprawling complex we see today. The palace complex covers approximately 240,000 square meters (2.6 million square feet) and contains over 2,600 rooms, making it one of the largest palaces in the world.

The architectural evolution of the Hofburg reflects the shifting tastes and political ambitions of the Habsburgs. The original Gothic elements of the palace are now overshadowed by later additions, including Renaissance, Baroque, Rococo, and Neoclassical elements. Each wing of the palace represents a different period in Austrian history, showcasing the dynasty's evolving relationship with power, culture, and art.

During the 19th century, the Hofburg became the primary residence of Emperor Franz Joseph I and his wife, Empress Elisabeth, better known as Sisi. It was during this period that the palace reached its zenith as the political, administrative, and ceremonial heart of the Austro-Hungarian Empire. Even after the collapse of the monarchy in 1918, the Hofburg remained a vital part of Austria's cultural and political life, transitioning from an imperial residence to a museum complex that houses some of the country's most important cultural treasures.

Architectural Highlights of the Hofburg Complex: The Hofburg's architectural layout is a fascinating reflection of the palace's layered history. Each wing or section of the palace complex has its own distinct character and historical significance. The main sections include:

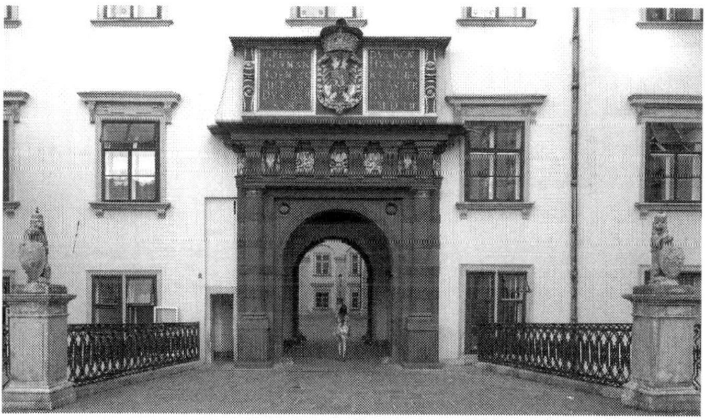

The Swiss Wing (Schweizerhof)

The Swiss Wing (Schweizerhof): The oldest part of the Hofburg, built in the 13th century, still retains elements of the medieval fortress, with the Swiss Gate being a prime example of Renaissance architecture.

The Amalienburg: Named after Empress Amalia, this Renaissance-style wing features an onion-domed tower, reflecting the Habsburgs' early Baroque influences.

The Leopold Wing: Built during the reign of Leopold I, this wing features grand Baroque interiors and now houses the Imperial Apartments.

The Michael Wing: A later addition to the palace, completed in the 19th century, the Michael Wing features a grand rotunda entrance and connects the palace to Michaelplatz.

The Neue Burg: The grandest of all the wings, constructed during the late 19th and early 20th centuries. This section now houses several museums and provides a sweeping view of Heldenplatz.

What to See: A Step-by-Step Guide

Visiting the Hofburg can be an overwhelming experience given its sheer size and the number of attractions housed within its walls. Here's a suggested itinerary that will take you through the most significant highlights of the complex, arranged in a logical order to ensure a smooth and enjoyable tour.

The Imperial Apartments (Kaiserappartements)

Estimated time: 1-1.5 hours

Start your visit with the Imperial Apartments, located in the Leopold Wing. These rooms were once the private quarters of Emperor Franz Joseph I and Empress Elisabeth (Sisi). The apartments are preserved in their original 19th-century décor and offer a glimpse into the daily life of the Habsburg court. The rooms are furnished with ornate Rococo furniture, crystal chandeliers, and intricate tapestries, all reflecting the imperial opulence of the Austro-Hungarian period.

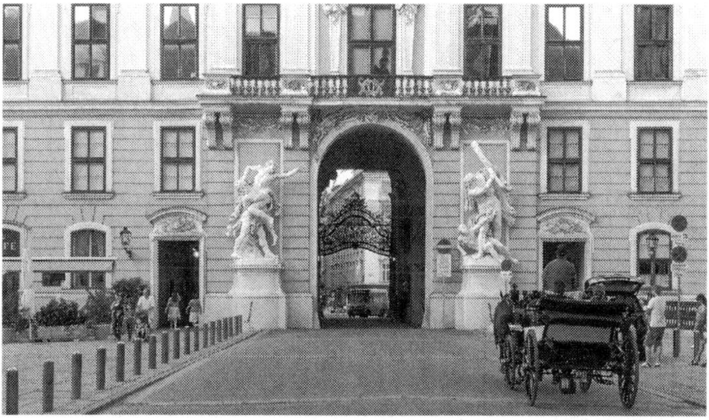

The Imperial Apartments

Kaiserliche Wohnungen | The Imperial Apartments

Address: Hofburg, 1010 Vienna

Public transport: U3 to Herrengasse

Opening hours: Daily: 10 a.m. – 5 p.m.

Online: www.sisimuseum-hofburg.at/en/

Highlights include:

Franz Joseph's Study: A more modestly decorated room where the emperor spent most of his working hours.

The Audience Chamber: Where the emperor received his guests, featuring portraits of important Habsburg family members.

Sisi's Salon: Empress Elisabeth's private rooms, including her dressing room and bedroom, filled with personal artifacts that offer insight into her mysterious and often melancholic life.

Curiosity: Empress Elisabeth was famously obsessed with beauty and fitness. Her apartments contain some of her exercise equipment, including a balance beam, which was highly unusual for the time.

The Sisi Museum

Estimated time: 1 hour

Next, head to the Sisi Museum, which is dedicated to the life of Empress Elisabeth, one of the most fascinating figures in Habsburg history. Known for her unconventional lifestyle, her beauty, and her tragic death, Sisi has become an icon in Austrian culture. The museum provides an intimate look at her life, showcasing personal items, including her dresses, jewelry and letters.

The museum delves into her complicated personality, exploring both her public and private personas. It also touches on her dislike of court life, her restless travels, and her obsession with maintaining her beauty, offering a nuanced portrayal of the famous empress.

Curiosity: Sisi's life was tragically cut short when she was assassinated in Geneva in 1898 by an Italian anarchist. A section of the museum is dedicated to this event, including the weapon used in the assassination.

Sisi Museum | Sisi Museum

Address: Hofburg, 1010 Vienna

Public transport: U3 to Herrengasse

Opening hours: Daily: 10 a.m. – 5 p.m.

Online: www.sisimuseum-hofburg.at/en/

The Silver Collection (Silberkammer)

Estimated time: 45 minutes - 1 hour

After the Sisi Museum, continue your exploration by visiting the Imperial Silver Collection, also located in the same area. This extensive collection showcases the elaborate tableware, cutlery, and dining sets used at the imperial court. The silver collection offers insight into the lavish banquets held at the Hofburg, where up to 500 people could be served at once.

Highlights include:

Exquisite porcelain from the imperial Vienna Porcelain Manufactory.

Gold and silver table settings, as well as centrepieces used for ceremonial dinners.

The famous Viennese court silver used by the Habsburgs, which reflects the craftsmanship of Austrian silversmiths.

Curiosity: The collection includes the 30-meter (98-foot) Milanese Centerpiece, which was used for official state banquets and features intricate depictions of mythological scenes.

Silberkammer | The Silver Collection

Address: Hofburg, 1010 Vienna

Public transport: U3 to Herrengasse

Opening hours: Daily: 10 a.m. – 5 p.m.

www.sisimuseum-hofburg.at/en/about-the-location/silver-collection

The Austrian National Library

Estimated time: 1 hour

The next stop is the Austrian National Library, located within the Baroque State Hall of the Hofburg. Built in the 18th century by Fischer von Erlach, this stunning hall is one of the most beautiful library spaces in the world. The grand, vaulted ceiling is adorned with frescoes by Daniel Gran, and the walls are lined with over 200,000 leather-bound books. The collection spans centuries, containing rare manuscripts, incunabula (books printed before 1501), and ancient maps.

Curiosity: The State Hall also contains statues of important Habsburg rulers, including Emperor Charles VI, who was the library's original patron. The central dome fresco depicts Charles VI as the bringer of wisdom and enlightenment to his people.

Österreichische Nationalbibliothek | The Austrian National Library

Address: Josefsplatz 1, 1010 Vienna

Public transport: U3 to Herrengasse

Opening hours: Tue-Sun: 10 a.m. – 6 p.m.; Thu: 10 a.m. – 9 p.m.; Mon: closed

Online: www.onb.ac.at/en/

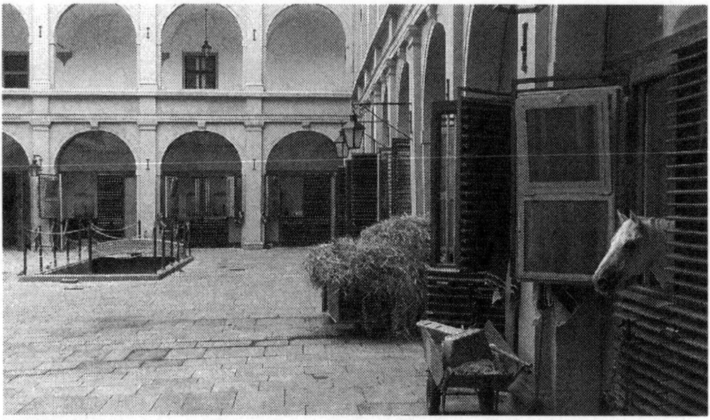

The Lipizzaner stables located in the Stallburg, adjacent to the Hofburg.

The Spanish Riding School (Spanische Hofreitschule)

Estimated time: 1-1.5 hours (depending on performance schedules)

A short walk from the library will take you to the world-famous Spanish Riding School, where you can witness the skill and precision of the Lipizzaner stallions. Founded in the 16th century, the riding school is one of the oldest of its kind in the world and is renowned for its classical dressage performances. The horses perform complex maneuvers, demonstrating the highest level of equestrian training.

Visitors can watch the morning training sessions, or, if available, attend a full performance in the Winter Riding Hall, an elegant Baroque arena built during the reign of Emperor Charles VI.

Curiosity: The Lipizzaner breed originated from a cross between Spanish, Italian, and Arab horses. Despite their dark birth color, the horses turn white as they mature.

Spanische Hofreitschule | The Spanish Riding School

Address: Michaelerplatz 1, 1010 Vienna

Public transport: U3 to Herrengasse

Opening hours: Performance times vary

Online: www.srs.at/en/

The Imperial Treasury (Schatzkammer)

Estimated time: 1-1.5 hours

Finally, conclude your visit to the Hofburg Palace with the Imperial Treasury, which houses some of the most priceless artifacts of the Habsburg monarchy.

The collection includes the Austrian Crown Jewels, which feature the Imperial Crown of Austria, the Holy Roman Emperor's crown, and other regalia used in coronations and state ceremonies.

The treasury also contains religious relics, including a fragment of the True Cross and the Holy Lance, believed to have been used during the crucifixion of Jesus Christ.

Other highlights include:

The Burgundian Treasure, a stunning collection of medieval tapestries, gold, and jewels.

The Napoleonic treasures, which belonged to Napoleon II, son of Napoleon Bonaparte and Marie Louise, daughter of Emperor Francis II of Austria.

Curiosity: The Imperial Treasury houses a unicorn horn, long believed to have magical powers, which is actually the tusk of a narwhal.

Schatzkammer | The Imperial Treasury

Address: Hofburg, Schweizerhof, 1010 Vienna

Public transport: U3 to Herrengasse

Opening hours: Daily: 9 a.m. – 5:30 p.m.

Online: www.kaiserliche-schatzkammer.at/en/

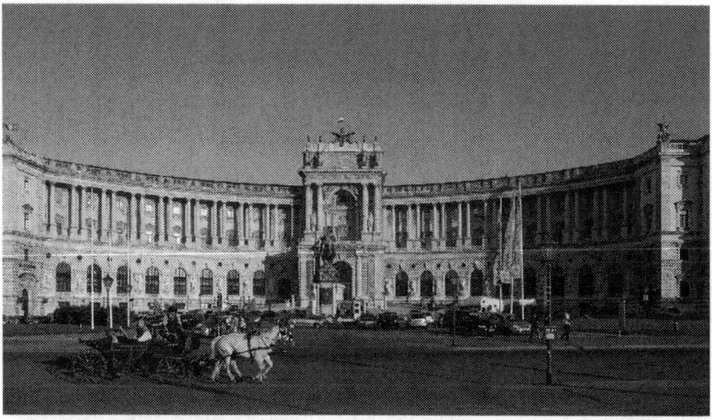

The New Wing of the Hofburg Palace, also known as the Neue Burg.

The Neue Burg: The New Wing of the Hofburg Palace, also known as the Neue Burg, is a late addition to Vienna's grand imperial complex, showcasing a blend of historicist architecture with Baroque and Classical influences. Construction began in 1881 as part of Emperor Franz Joseph's ambitious plan to expand the palace and create a monumental setting for the Habsburg monarchy.

However, the Neue Burg was only completed in 1913, shortly before the collapse of the empire. It was originally intended to serve as additional living quarters for the imperial family and to house military and state offices.

Today, the New Wing is home to several important museums, including the Weltmuseum, the Imperial Armoury, and the Ephesos Museum, blending the rich history of the Habsburg era with modern cultural exhibitions.

Papyrus Museum

Estimated time: 1 hour

The Papyrus Museum in the New Wing of the Hofburg houses one of the world's most extensive collections of ancient papyri, offering a rare glimpse into daily life, religion, and administration in ancient Egypt and the Middle East. The collection includes over 180,000 papyrus fragments, some dating back over 3,000 years, and covers topics like medical texts, legal documents, and personal letters. Visitors can explore the fascinating world of ancient writing and its role in shaping early civilizations.

Papyrusmuseum | Papyrus Museum

Address: Neue Burg, 1010 Vienna, Austria

Public transport: U-Bahn lines U3 to Herrengasse

Opening hours: Daily 10 a.m. – 6 p.m.; closed on monday

www.onb.ac.at/en/museums/papyrus-museum

Ephesos Museum

Estimated time: 1 hour

The Ephesos Museum showcases a rich collection of archaeological finds from the ancient city of Ephesus, one of the most important cities of the Roman Empire. Highlights include marble statues, reliefs, and architectural elements, giving insight into the grandeur of Ephesus. Visitors can explore artifacts from the Temple of Artemis, one of the Seven Wonders of the Ancient World, as well as items illustrating the daily lives of the ancient city's residents.

Ephesos Museum | Ephesos Museum

Address: Neue Burg, 1010 Vienna, Austria

Public transport: U-Bahn lines U3 to Herrengasse

Opening hours: Daily 10 a.m. – 6 p.m.

www.khm.at/en/visit/collections/ephesos-museum/

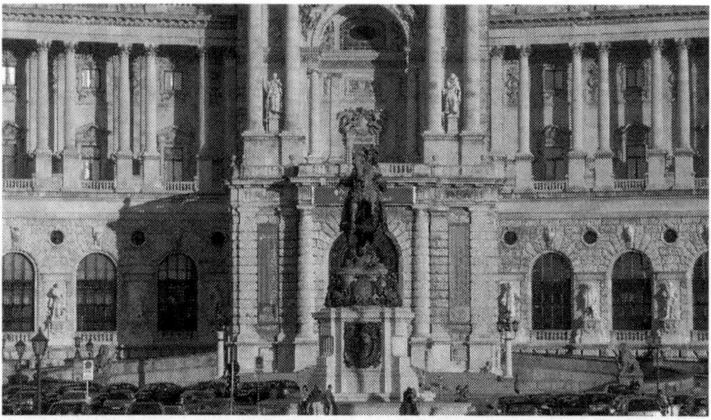

Prince Eugene on horseback stands before the main entrance of the Neue Burg and its museums

The Imperial Armoury

Estimated time: 1 hour

The Imperial Armoury (Hofjagd- und Rüstkammer) features one of the most significant collections of historical arms and armor in the world.

Dating from the 15th to the 19th centuries, the collection includes ornate suits of armor, weapons, and tournament gear that once belonged to the Habsburg rulers.

This museum offers a fascinating insight into the military history of the Habsburg Empire and the craftsmanship behind these elaborate, functional works of art.

Hofjagd- und Rüstkammer | Imperial Armoury

Address: Neue Burg, 1010 Vienna, Austria

Public transport: U-Bahn lines U3 to Herrengasse

Opening hours: Daily 10 a.m. – 6 p.m.

www.khm.at/en/visit/collections/imperial-armoury/

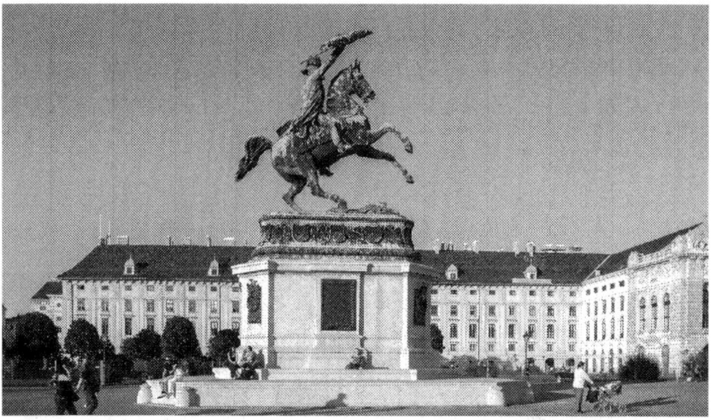

The equestrian monument honors Archduke Karl, the first to deliver Napoleon a significant military defeat.

Collection of Old Musical Instruments

Estimated time: 1 hour

The Collection of Old Musical Instruments displays a vast array of historical instruments, many of which were used by renowned composers like Mozart, Beethoven, and Haydn.

The collection covers over five centuries of European music history, featuring instruments such as harpsichords, violins, and early pianos. Visitors can see rare and beautifully crafted instruments that were central to the development of Western classical music.

Sammlung alter Musikinstrumente | Collection of Old Musical Instruments

Address: Neue Burg, 1010 Vienna, Austria

Public transport: U-Bahn lines U3 to Herrengasse

Opening hours: Daily 10 a.m. – 6 p.m.

www.khm.at/en/visit/collections/collection-of-historic-musical-instruments/

Weltmuseum Wien (World Museum)

Estimated time: 1-1.5 hours

The Weltmuseum Wien (World Museum) is one of the leading ethnographic museums in the world, housing over 200,000 objects from cultures across the globe. The museum's collections include artifacts from Asia, Africa, Oceania, and the Americas, with highlights such as the famous feathered headdress from Mexico and ancient African sculptures. The exhibits explore the diversity of human cultures and history, focusing on the art, spirituality, and everyday life of different civilizations.

Weltmuseum Wien | World Museum

Address: Neue Burg, 1010 Vienna, Austria

Public transport: U-Bahn lines U3 to Herrengasse

Opening hours: Daily 10 a.m. – 6 p.m.

Online: www.weltmuseumwien.at/en/

Kunsthistorisches Museum

Walking distance from Hofburg Palace: 700 meters / 0.43 miles

Walking time: 9-10 minutes

Kunsthistorisches Museum | Kunsthistorisches Museum

Address: Maria-Theresien-Platz, 1010 Vienna

Public transport: U2 to Museumsquartier

Opening hours: Daily: 10 a.m. – 6 p.m.; Thu: 10 a.m. – 9 p.m.

Online: www.khm.at/en/

One of the world's finest art museums, the Kunsthistorisches Museum was built in the Neo-Renaissance style to house the Habsburgs' vast art collection. The grand staircase and dome are architectural masterpieces. Inside, you'll find works by European masters like Bruegel, Raphael, Velázquez, and Titian.

Curiosity: Across from the museum, you will find the Naturhistorisches Museum (Natural History Museum), an architectural twin that also features a striking dome and grand staircases.

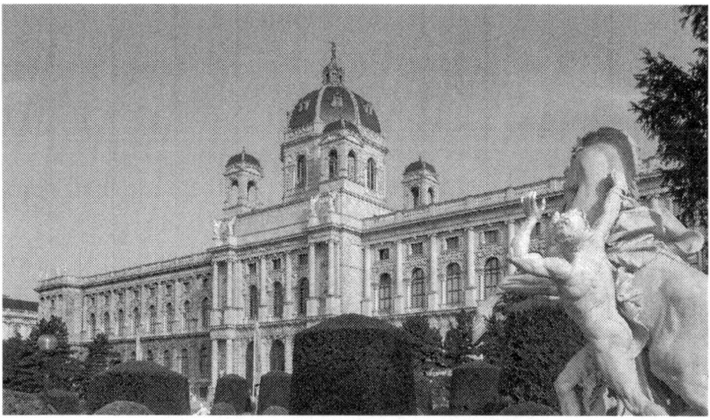

Kunsthistorisches Museum (KHM)

The Kunsthistorisches Museum (Museum of Art History) is not only one of Vienna's premier cultural institutions but also one of the most important art museums in the world. Located on Maria-Theresien-Platz, the museum houses an extraordinary collection of art spanning millennia, from ancient Egyptian artifacts to Renaissance masterpieces and Baroque treasures. Built in the late 19th century during the reign of Emperor Franz Joseph I, the museum was designed to display the vast art collections of the Habsburg dynasty, showcasing the cultural wealth and power of the Austrian Empire.

Designed in the Neo-Renaissance style by architects Gottfried Semper and Karl von Hasenauer, the Kunsthistorisches Museum is itself a masterpiece of architecture. Its grandeur and symmetry reflect the spirit of the Habsburg era, making the building as much of a cultural monument as the works of art it contains. Inside, visitors are greeted with stunning marble staircases, ornate ceilings, and grand exhibition halls that provide an opulent setting for some of the greatest works of Western art.

We will explore the architectural and historical significance of the Kunsthistorisches Museum, providing a detailed guide on what to see during your visit. From ancient Egyptian treasures to Renaissance paintings by Raphael, Bruegel, and Velázquez, the museum offers a journey through the evolution of art and civilization. We'll also explore the surrounding area of Maria-Theresien-Platz, where cultural and historical landmarks abound.

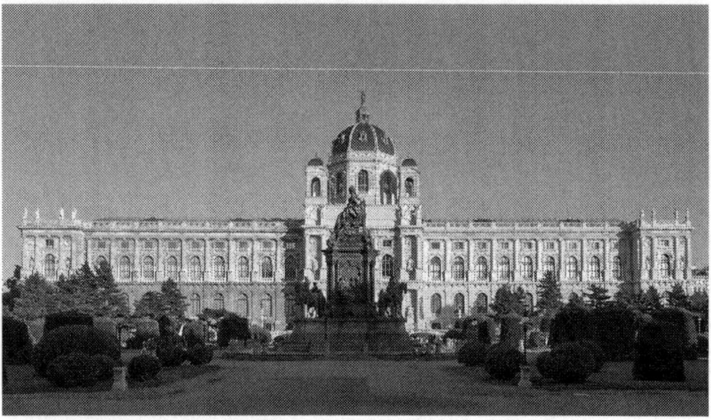

The Kunsthistorisches Museum is located on Maria Theresa Square.

Historical Overview: The Kunsthistorisches Museum was built to house the extensive art collections of the Habsburgs, one of Europe's most powerful dynasties. For centuries, the Habsburg emperors were patrons of the arts, collecting works from across Europe and beyond. By the 19th century, the collection had grown so large that it required a dedicated museum space to properly display the treasures accumulated over centuries of Habsburg rule.

Construction of the museum began in 1871, and it was officially opened in 1891 by Emperor Franz Joseph I. The museum was part of the broader development of the Ringstrasse, a grand boulevard encircling the historic center of Vienna, which was designed to showcase the city's imperial grandeur. The Kunsthistorisches Museum was built opposite its twin, the Naturhistorisches Museum (Museum of Natural History), creating a harmonious architectural ensemble on Maria-Theresien-Platz.

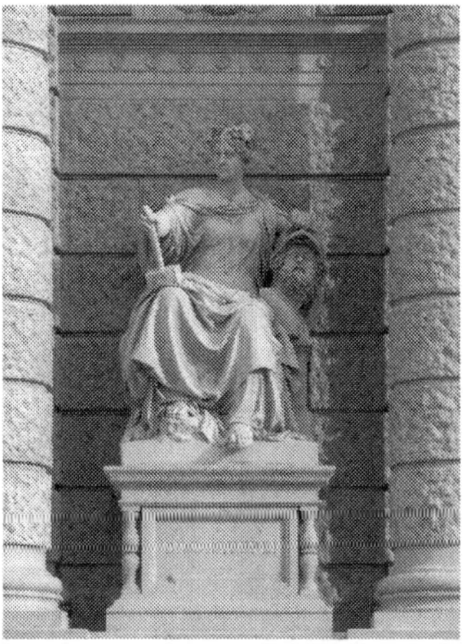

Allegory of Sculpture displayed on the museum's facade.

The building's Neo-Renaissance style reflects the Habsburgs' desire to connect their reign with the cultural achievements of the past, particularly the Renaissance, a period that emphasized humanism, science, and artistic innovation. Inside, the museum was designed to impress visitors with its grand staircases, soaring ceilings, and lavish decoration, creating a fitting setting for one of the world's greatest art collections.

Architectural Highlights: The Kunsthistorisches Museum's architectural grandeur is immediately apparent from the moment you approach the building. The museum's symmetrical façade, with its monumental columns, pediments, and domed roof, is a masterpiece of Neo-Renaissance design. The richly decorated interior is equally impressive, featuring a central rotunda, grand staircases, and frescoes by Gustav Klimt and his brothers, Ernst Klimt and Georg Klimt.

Key architectural features include:

The Main Façade: The museum's main entrance is framed by Corinthian columns and topped with a grand pediment, which is adorned with allegorical figures representing the arts and sciences. The façade is designed to convey the cultural and intellectual ambitions of the Habsburgs, with inscriptions celebrating the museum's role in preserving and displaying the empire's artistic heritage.

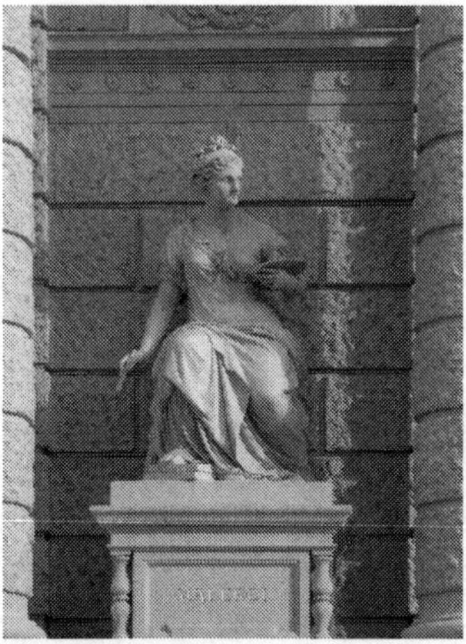

Allegory of Painting, to the left of the entrance.

The Dome: The central dome, rising 60 meters (197 feet) above the rotunda, is one of the most striking features of the building. The dome symbolizes the universality of art and knowledge, reflecting the Habsburgs' desire to create a museum that would rival the great cultural institutions of Europe.

The Grand Staircase: Inside the museum, the grand staircase is one of the most impressive architectural elements. Made of marble and adorned with statues and frescoes, the staircase leads visitors to the upper galleries. Look for the ceiling frescoes, painted by Mihály Munkácsy, which depict the triumph of civilization through art.

The Klimt Friezes: Before you ascend the grand staircase, take a moment to admire the friezes on the walls, which were created by Gustav Klimt, Ernst Klimt, and Georg Klimt. These friezes depict figures from classical mythology and allegories of the arts, offering an early glimpse of Gustav Klimt's later, more famous works.

Inside the Museum: A Step-by-Step Guide

The Kunsthistorisches Museum's vast collection is divided into several departments, each dedicated to a specific period or type of art.

To make the most of your visit, follow this step-by-step guide, which highlights the museum's most important treasures.

The Picture Gallery

Estimated time: 1.5-2 hours

Begin your visit in the Picture Gallery, which is home to one of the world's finest collections of European paintings from the 15th to the 18th centuries. The gallery is organized by national schools, with works by Italian, Flemish, Dutch, and Spanish masters.

Key highlights include:

Pieter Bruegel the Elder: The museum holds the largest collection of works by Bruegel in the world, including his famous painting "Hunters in the Snow" (1565), part of a series of seasonal landscapes. This painting is a masterpiece of Northern Renaissance art, depicting a serene winter scene that captures the everyday life of peasants.

Raphael: The Madonna of the Meadow (1505-1506) is one of Raphael's most celebrated works. This painting, with its harmonious composition and delicate use of color, exemplifies the ideals of the High Renaissance.

Titian: The Venetian master Titian is well represented in the collection. His "Portrait of Isabella d'Este" (1534-1536) is a striking depiction of one of the most powerful women of the Renaissance, known for her patronage of the arts.

Velázquez: The Spanish Golden Age painter Diego Velázquez is another highlight of the museum's collection. His "Infanta Margarita Teresa in a Blue Dress" (1659) is a stunning portrait of the young Habsburg princess, capturing both her innocence and her regal status.

Curiosity: In addition to Bruegel's winter scene, his painting "The Tower of Babel" (1563) is another must-see. This highly detailed depiction of the biblical story is filled with tiny figures and architectural marvels that reflect Bruegel's fascination with human ambition and folly.

The Egyptian and Near Eastern Collection

Estimated time: 45 minutes - 1 hour

Next, move on to the Egyptian and Near Eastern Collection, one of the oldest and most comprehensive collections of Egyptian art in Europe. The collection spans more than 3,000 years of history, offering a fascinating glimpse into the religious and funerary practices of ancient Egypt.

Highlights include:

Sarcophagi and Mummies: The museum's collection of sarcophagi and mummies is a highlight of the Egyptian section. The intricately painted coffins and preserved mummies offer insight into the Egyptian belief in the afterlife and the rituals associated with death and burial.

Statuary and Reliefs: The collection includes a wide range of statuary and reliefs, depicting gods, pharaohs, and everyday people. Look for the statue of Pharaoh Thutmose III, one of Egypt's greatest military leaders, as well as the limestone reliefs from the tombs of Egyptian nobles.

The Book of the Dead: One of the most fascinating artifacts in the collection is a section of the Book of the Dead, a series of funerary texts intended to guide the deceased through the afterlife. The hieroglyphs and illustrations provide valuable insight into ancient Egyptian religious beliefs.

Curiosity: The collection also includes an Assyrian relief from the palace of King Ashurnasirpal II in Nimrud, depicting a winged genius. This piece reflects the artistic and religious traditions of ancient Mesopotamia, offering a glimpse into the cultures of the Near East.

The Greek and Roman Antiquities

Estimated time: 45 minutes

From Egypt, travel through time to the world of classical antiquity in the Greek and Roman Collection. This section of the museum contains statues, pottery, and jewelry from ancient Greece and Rome, showcasing the artistic achievements of these great civilizations.

Highlights include:

The Youth from Magdalensberg: This bronze statue of a young man, dating from the 1st century BC, is one of the finest examples of Roman sculpture in the museum. The statue was discovered in Austria and is believed to have been created by a Roman artist during the early days of Roman rule in the region.

Greek Pottery: The collection features a stunning array of Greek vases, including examples of both black figure and red figure pottery. These vases depict scenes from mythology, daily life, and athletic competitions, offering a window into ancient Greek culture.

Roman Portrait Busts: The museum also holds an impressive collection of Roman portrait busts, including depictions of emperors, philosophers, and other important figures from Roman history.

Curiosity: One of the most intriguing artifacts in this collection is a Roman glass bowl that changes color depending on the angle of light. This effect, known as dichroism, was achieved by mixing tiny particles of gold and silver into the glass, creating a magical effect that astonishes visitors even today.

The Kunstkammer

Estimated time: 1-1.5 hours

The Kunstkammer is one of the most unique sections of the museum, housing the Habsburgs' collection of curiosities, treasures, and rare objects. This collection, also known as the Chamber of Art and

Wonders, reflects the Habsburgs' fascination with the exotic, the unusual, and the marvelous.

Highlights include:

Benvenuto Cellini's Salt Cellar: One of the most famous items in the Kunstkammer is Benvenuto Cellini's Salt Cellar (1540-1543), a magnificent gold and enamel sculpture that depicts the gods Neptune and Terra. This Renaissance masterpiece is one of the most important works of decorative art in the world.

Mechanical Automata: The Kunstkammer contains several mechanical automata, including elaborate clocks and mechanical birds that were designed to entertain the Habsburg court. These items showcase the ingenuity of Renaissance and Baroque craftsmen.

Ivory Carvings: The collection includes a stunning array of ivory carvings, including delicate miniature sculptures of saints, mythological figures, and animals. The skill and precision required to create these intricate works is truly remarkable.

Curiosity: The Kunstkammer also contains a collection of **coral sculptures**, which were believed to have protective and healing properties in the Renaissance. These sculptures, often depicting religious scenes, were highly prized by collectors.

The Coin Collection

Estimated time: 30-45 minutes

Finally, don't miss the museum's Coin Collection, one of the largest and most comprehensive in the world. The collection spans from ancient times to the modern era, with coins, medals, and currency from civilizations around the globe.

Highlights include:

Greek and Roman Coins: The collection contains rare examples of ancient Greek and Roman coins, including gold staters, silver denarii, and bronze sestertii. These coins offer valuable insights into the political and economic history of the classical world.

Medieval and Renaissance Medals: The museum also holds an impressive collection of medieval and Renaissance medals, including pieces commissioned by European rulers to commemorate important events. These medals are often highly detailed, with portraits and allegorical scenes engraved on their surfaces.

Curiosity: The collection includes a gold coin minted during the reign of Charlemagne, one of the earliest examples of European coinage. This rare artifact reflects the political and economic power of the Holy Roman Empire.

Exploring the Surrounding Area

Once you've explored the Kunsthistorisches Museum, take some time to enjoy the beautiful surroundings of Maria-Theresien-Platz, a grand square that connects the museum to its twin, the Naturhistorisches Museum.

Maria-Theresien-Platz

The square is dominated by the imposing Maria Theresa Monument, a grand statue of Empress Maria Theresa, who ruled the Habsburg Empire in the 18th century.

The monument, completed in 1888, features the empress seated on a throne, surrounded by generals, statesmen, and scholars who contributed to the empire's success.

Curiosity: Maria Theresa was one of the most powerful women in European history, known for her reforms in education, healthcare, and the military.

The monument reflects her legacy as a ruler who modernized the Habsburg Empire.

The Naturhistorisches Museum

Estimated time: 2 hours

Directly across from the Kunsthistorisches Museum is the Naturhistorisches Museum (Museum of Natural History), which was designed as a twin to the art museum. The two buildings are almost identical in their Neo-Renaissance design, creating a harmonious architectural ensemble on Maria-Theresien-Platz. The Naturhistorisches Museum houses an extraordinary collection of minerals, fossils, dinosaur skeletons, and meteorites.

Curiosity: The museum is home to the famous Venus of Willendorf, a small prehistoric figurine that is over 25,000 years old and is considered one of the most important archaeological discoveries in Austria.

Naturhistorisches Museum | Museum of Natural History

Address: Maria-Theresien-Platz, 1010 Vienna

Public transport: U2 to Museumsquartier

Opening hours: Thu-Mon: 9 a.m. – 6:30 p.m.; Wed: 9 a.m. – 9 p.m.; Tue: closed

Online: www.nhm-wien.ac.at/en

Secession Building

Walking distance: 1.2 kilometers / 0.75 miles

Walking time: 14-16 minutes

Secessionsgebäude | The Secession Building

Address: Friedrichstraße 12, 1010 Vienna

Public transport: U1, U2, U4 to Karlsplatz

Opening hours: Tue-Sun: 10:00 – 18:00

Online: https://secession.at/

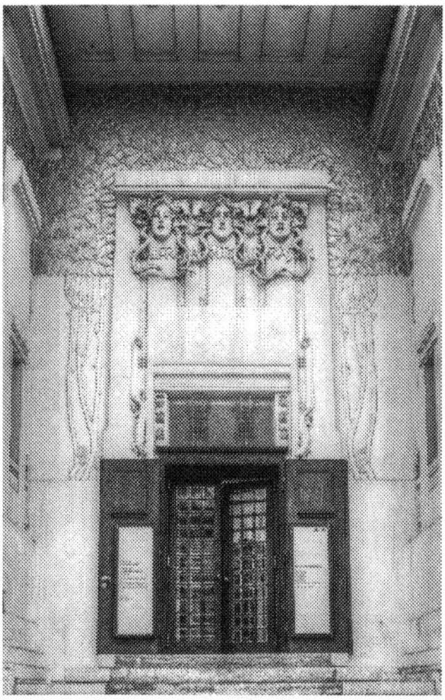

The Secession Building

The Secession Building is a striking Art Nouveau structure designed by Joseph Maria Olbrich in 1897 as the headquarters of the Vienna Secession movement. Its white, minimalist exterior is topped with a golden dome of laurel leaves, nicknamed the "golden cabbage." Inside, you can view Gustav Klimt's famous Beethoven Frieze, a manifestation of the bold, modernist spirit of turn-of-the-century Vienna.

Curiosity: Nearby, you'll find the Naschmarkt, Vienna's most famous market, where you can stop for a snack, offering a variety of local and international foods.

Lunch break suggestion: Head over to the Naschmarkt for some Austrian specialties such as Wiener Schnitzel or pastries like Apfelstrudel.

The Secession Building in Vienna is one of the most recognizable landmarks of the Art Nouveau (Jugendstil) movement, embodying the radical spirit of artistic innovation at the turn of the 20th century. Built in 1897 by Joseph Maria Olbrich as the headquarters for the Vienna Secession, the building is a bold rejection of the conservative artistic traditions that dominated the Viennese cultural scene in the late 19th century. The Vienna Secession, a group of avant-garde artists including Gustav Klimt, Koloman Moser, and Josef Hoffmann, sought to break free from the constraints of academic art and create new, modern forms of expression.

The Secession Building, with its stark white façade, golden dome of laurel leaves, and minimalistic design, was a radical departure from the heavily ornamented historicist styles that surrounded it. Today, the building remains a symbol of the Secessionists' mission to create an art that was "for every age its art, and for art its freedom," a phrase inscribed above the entrance. The building houses Klimt's Beethoven Frieze, one of the most important works of the period, and continues to be a center for contemporary art exhibitions.

We will explore the historical and architectural significance of the Secession Building, its role in the broader context of the Vienna Secession movement, and provide a guide on what to see during your visit, including nearby attractions that complement the Secession experience.

The Birth of the Vienna Secession: The Vienna Secession was founded in 1897 by a group of young, progressive artists who were dissatisfied with the conservative atmosphere of the Vienna Künstlerhaus, the city's dominant artistic institution. The Künstlerhaus, which adhered to the principles of historicism and academic art, favored works that were traditional in style and subject matter. However, a new generation of artists, influenced by the Symbolist and Art Nouveau movements sweeping through Europe, sought to explore more modern, abstract, and individualistic forms of expression.

Led by Gustav Klimt, the founding members of the Secession included painters, sculptors, and architects such as Koloman Moser, Carl Moll, Max Kurzweil, Josef Hoffmann, and Joseph Maria Olbrich. Their goal was to break away from the established artistic norms and create a space where they could exhibit works that reflected the changing social, cultural, and intellectual climate of the late 19th and early 20th centuries.

The Secessionists believed that art should not be confined to historical styles or academic traditions. Instead, it should reflect the unique spirit of the age, addressing contemporary issues such as industrialization, urbanization, and the psychological complexities of modern life. The group's slogan, inscribed above the entrance to the Secession Building, reflects this philosophy: "Der Zeit ihre Kunst, der Kunst ihre Freiheit" (To every age its art, to art its freedom).

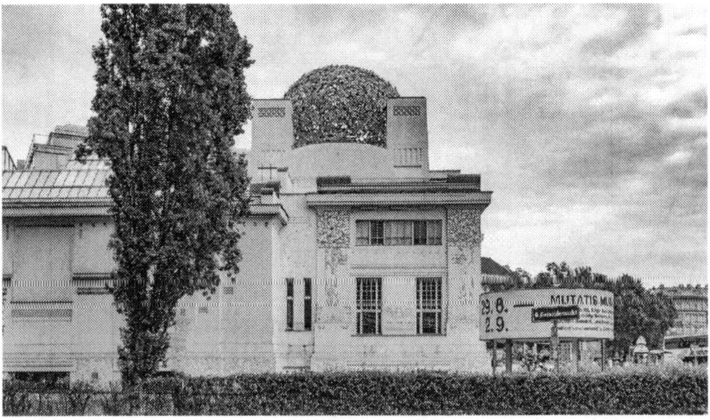

The Secession Building

In 1897, the city of Vienna granted the Secessionists permission to construct their own exhibition hall, and the result was the Secession Building, designed by the architect Joseph Maria Olbrich. The building was a radical departure from the traditional exhibition halls of the time, embodying the ideals of the Art Nouveau movement with its emphasis on geometric forms, natural motifs, and symbolic ornamentation.

Architectural Significance: The Secession Building is a striking example of Art Nouveau architecture, characterized by its clean lines, geometric shapes, and minimal ornamentation. The building's design reflects the Secessionists' rejection of the ornate historicism that dominated Viennese architecture in the late 19th century. Instead of the elaborate façades, arches, and columns typical of Neo-Baroque and Neo-Renaissance buildings, the Secession Building is stark and modern, with an emphasis on simplicity and abstraction.

Key architectural features include:

The Golden Dome: Perhaps the most iconic feature of the Secession Building is its golden dome, made of 3,000 gilded laurel leaves. The dome, often referred to as the "golden cabbage" by locals due to its shape, symbolizes victory, triumph, and artistic achievement. It also represents the Secessionists' break from tradition and their embrace of new, modern forms of artistic expression.

The White Façade: The building's white stucco façade is adorned with minimal ornamentation, a stark contrast to the richly decorated façades of other buildings in Vienna at the time. The simplicity of the design reflects the Secessionists' belief in the purity of form and the importance of artistic freedom.

The Entrance Reliefs: Above the entrance to the building are three gilded owls, symbols of wisdom, flanked by laurel wreaths. The building's entrance is further adorned with inscriptions that convey the group's philosophical ideals: "Der Zeit ihre Kunst, der Kunst ihre Freiheit".

Natural Motifs: Art Nouveau is known for its use of organic forms and natural motifs, and the Secession Building incorporates these elements into its design. The building's entrance features stylized floral reliefs and tendrils, symbolizing growth, creativity, and the natural world.

The interior of the Secession Building is designed to be flexible and adaptable, with large, open exhibition spaces that can accommodate a wide range of artistic displays. This focus on functionality and adaptability reflects the Secessionists' desire to create a space where artists from different disciplines could come together to exhibit their work.

Curiosity: The building's radical design sparked controversy when it was first unveiled, with many critics decrying its stark, modern appearance. However, it quickly became a symbol of the avant-garde movement and is now one of Vienna's most beloved landmarks.

What to See Inside: A Step-by-Step Guide

The Secession Building is both a historical monument and a contemporary art space. The most famous work housed within the building is Gustav Klimt's Beethoven Frieze, a masterpiece of early 20th-century art. However, the building also hosts rotating exhibitions of contemporary art, making it a dynamic space that continues to reflect the Secessionists' commitment to artistic innovation.

Klimt's Beethoven Frieze

Estimated time: 20 minutes

One of the most important works on display at the Secession Building is Gustav Klimt's Beethoven Frieze, created for the 14th Secessionist exhibition in 1902. The frieze is an allegorical depiction of humanity's quest for happiness, inspired by Ludwig van Beethoven's Ninth Symphony. Klimt's use of symbolism, eroticism, and decorative elements in the frieze represents the Secessionists' desire to merge fine art with applied arts, creating a "total work of art" (Gesamtkunstwerk).

The frieze is divided into several sections, each representing different stages of the human struggle for happiness. The leftmost section, titled "The Longing for Happiness", depicts a group of figures searching for love and contentment. The central section, "The Hostile Forces", features mythical creatures and monsters representing human suffering and obstacles. The rightmost section, "The Chorus of Angels", concludes with a depiction of lovers embracing, symbolizing the triumph of love and the attainment of spiritual peace.

Curiosity: Klimt's frieze was originally intended to be a temporary installation, created specifically for the 1902 exhibition. However, it was preserved in the Secession Building's lower gallery, where it remains one of the most important works of the Art Nouveau period.

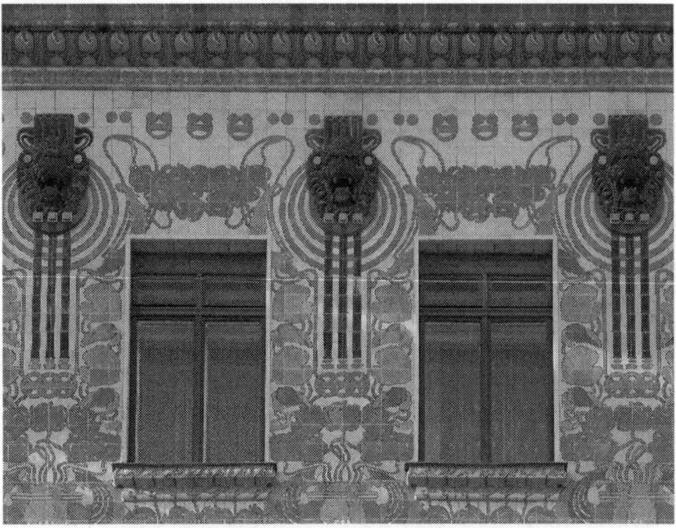

The Majolica House by Otto Wagner

Exploring the Surrounding Area

The Secession Building is located in the vibrant district of Karlsplatz, which is home to several other important cultural landmarks and attractions. After visiting the Secession Building, take some time to explore the surrounding area, which offers a mix of historical architecture, modern art, and bustling market life.

Naschmarkt

Location: Linke Wienzeile

Walking distance: 500 meters / 0.31 miles

Walking time: 6-7 minutes

Just a few minutes' walk from the Secession Building is the Naschmarkt, Vienna's most famous open-air market. The Naschmarkt is a vibrant hub of activity, offering a wide variety of fresh produce, international foods, and local delicacies. It's a great place to stop for lunch or a snack after exploring the Secession Building.

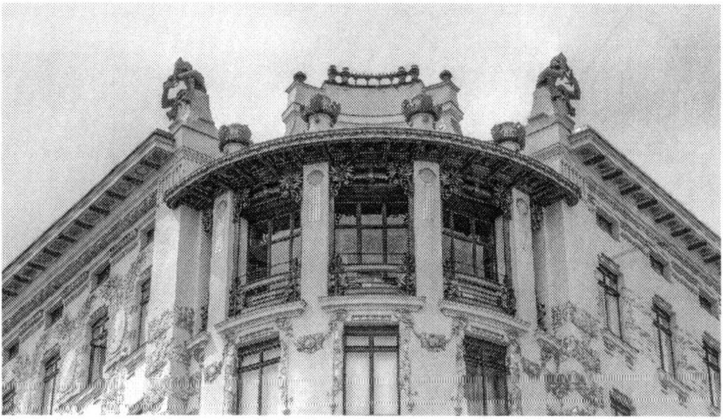

The House of the Medallions by Otto Wagner

The market is also a hotspot for Art Nouveau architecture, with several buildings designed by Otto Wagner lining the Linke Wienzeile. Wagner, another prominent figure of the Vienna Secession, left a lasting mark on the city's architectural landscape with his innovative designs.

The Majolica House and the House of the Medallions, two of Otto Wagner's most famous Art Nouveau buildings, are located along the Naschmarkt.

Karlskirche (St. Charles's Church)

Location: Karlsplatz

Walking distance: 400 meters / 0.25 miles

Walking time: 5 minutes

Just a short walk from the Secession Building is the Karlskirche, one of Vienna's most famous Baroque churches.

Designed by Johann Bernhard Fischer von Erlach and completed in 1737, the church is known for its grand dome and twin columns, which are modeled after Trajan's Column in Rome. Inside, the church features stunning frescoes and a magnificent altar. Visitors can take an elevator up to the dome's interior, where they can admire the frescoes up close and enjoy panoramic views of the city.

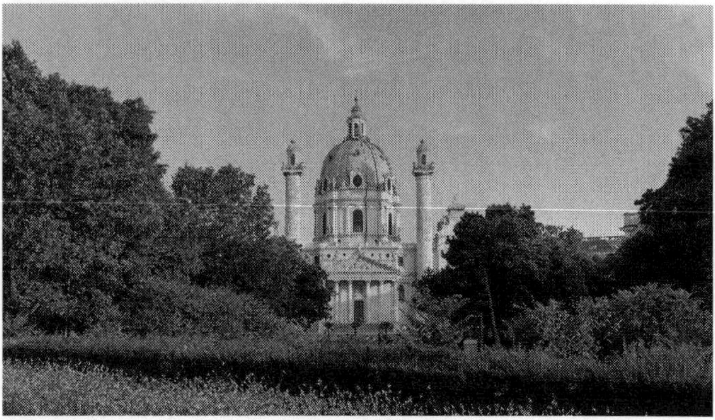

St. Charles's Church

Karlskirche | St. Charles's Church

Address: Karlsplatz, 1040 Vienna

Public transport: U1, U2, U4 to Karlsplatz

Opening hours: Mon-Sat: 9 a.m. – 6 p.m.; Sun: 12 p.m. – 7 p.m.

Online: www.karlskirche.at

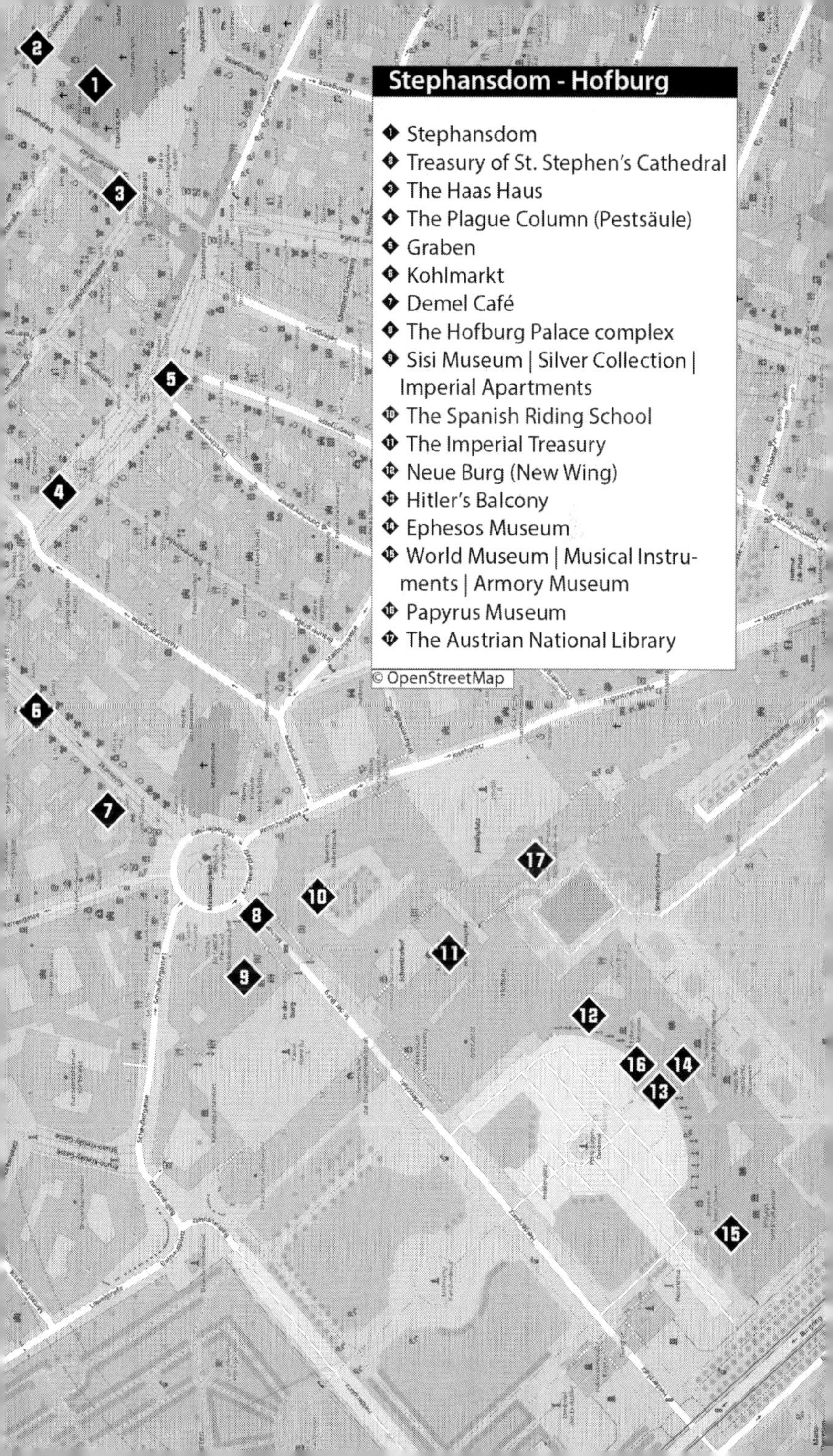
Stephansdom - Hofburg
1 Stephansdom
2 Treasury of St. Stephen's Cathedral
3 The Haas Haus
4 The Plague Column (Pestsäule)
5 Graben
6 Kohlmarkt
7 Demel Café
8 The Hofburg Palace complex
9 Sisi Museum | Silver Collection | Imperial Apartments
10 The Spanish Riding School
11 The Imperial Treasury
12 Neue Burg (New Wing)
13 Hitler's Balcony
14 Ephesos Museum
15 World Museum | Musical Instruments | Armory Museum
16 Papyrus Museum
17 The Austrian National Library
© OpenStreetMap

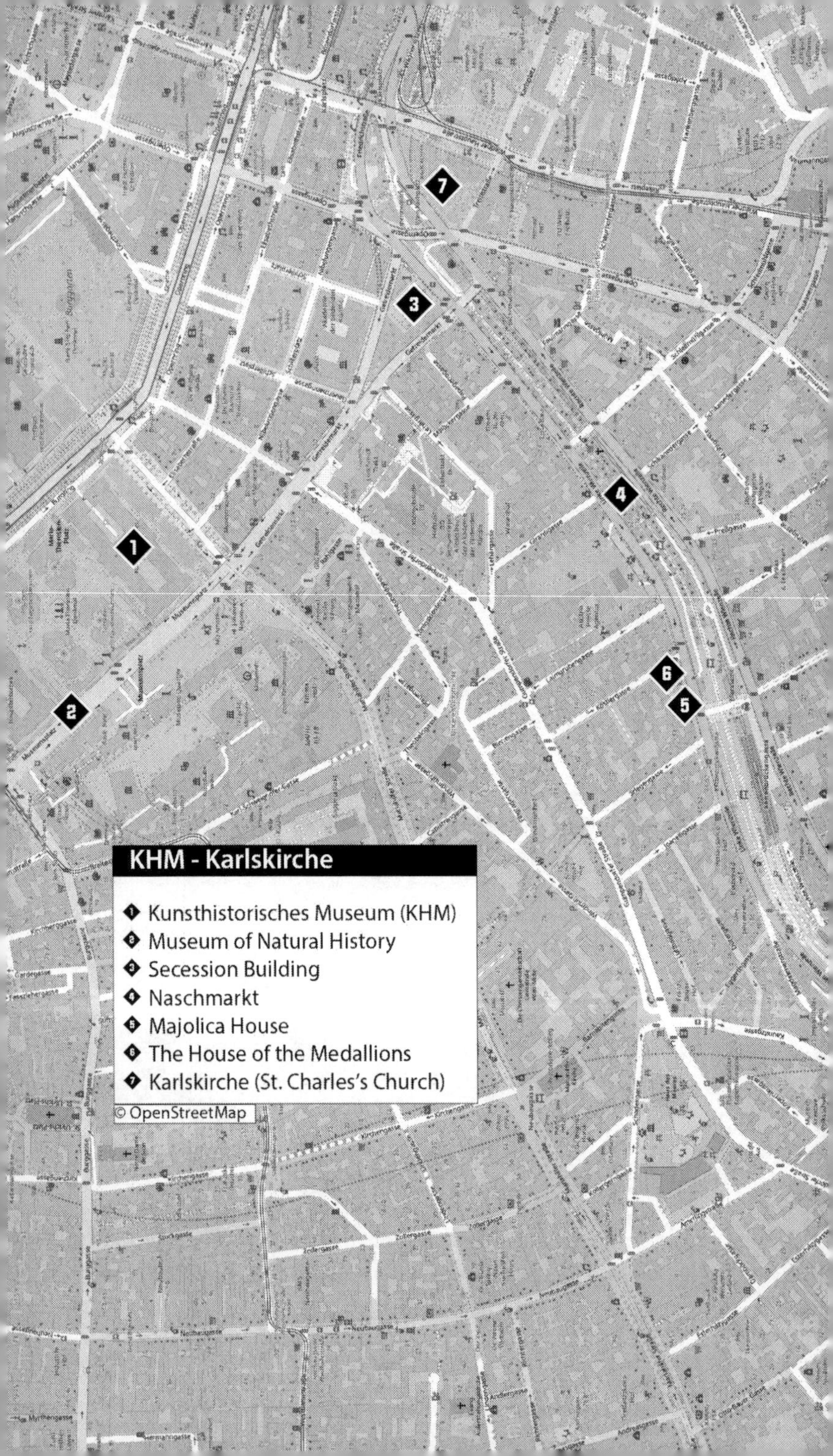
1
2
3
4
5
6
7
KHM - Karlskirche
1 Kunsthistorisches Museum (KHM)
2 Museum of Natural History
3 Secession Building
4 Naschmarkt
5 Majolica House
6 The House of the Medallions
7 Karlskirche (St. Charles's Church)
© OpenStreetMap

OLD TOWN WALK – ART AND GLORY

Belvedere Palace complex

Location: Prinz Eugen-Straße 27, 1030 Vienna

Public transport: U1 to Hauptbahnhof, then tram D to Schloss Belvedere

Walking distance: 1.2 kilometers / 0.75 miles

Walking time: 18-20 minutes

Schloss Belvedere | Belvedere Palace

Address: Prinz Eugen-Straße 27, 1030 Vienna

Public transport: Tram D to Schloss Belvedere

Opening hours: Daily: 10 a.m. – 6 p.m.

Online: www.belvedere.at/en

After lunch, make your way to the Belvedere Palace, a Baroque masterpiece designed by Johann Lukas von Hildebrandt. The palace is divided into the Upper and Lower Belvedere, set within beautiful gardens.

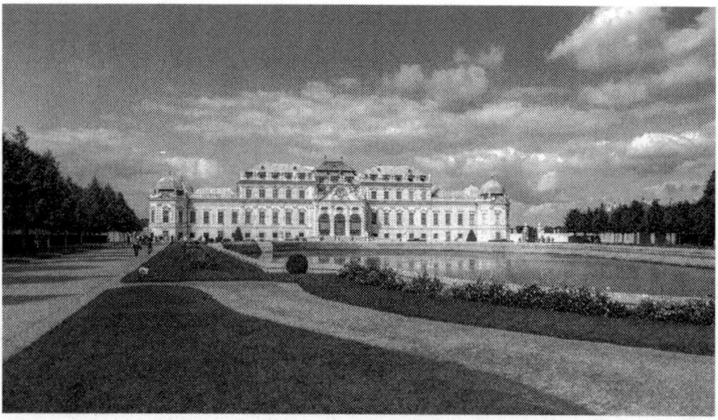

The Upper Belvedere

It houses the world's largest collection of works by Gustav Klimt, including his masterpiece *The Kiss*, as well as important works by Egon Schiele and Oskar Kokoschka.

Curiosity: The gardens between the two palaces are not only a stunning example of Baroque landscaping but also feature a hidden pond that mirrors the palace.

The Belvedere Palace is one of Vienna's most iconic and beautiful landmarks, an outstanding example of Baroque architecture set within magnificent gardens that offer panoramic views of the city. Originally constructed as a summer residence for Prince Eugene of Savoy, the Belvedere Palace complex is now home to the Belvedere Museum, which houses one of Austria's most important collections of fine art, including the world's largest collection of works by Gustav Klimt, such as the world-renowned *The Kiss.* The Belvedere, with its elegant palaces and expansive gardens, represents the height of Baroque design and is a UNESCO World Heritage Site.

The palace complex is divided into two main buildings: the Upper Belvedere and the Lower Belvedere, which are connected by formal French-style gardens. While the Upper Belvedere is known for its grand architecture and houses the museum's most famous paintings, the Lower Belvedere contains intimate salons and the Orangery, which host temporary exhibitions. The Palace Stables, another part of the complex, showcase medieval art, while the extensive gardens and fountains are works of art in themselves, reflecting the grandeur and symmetry of Baroque landscaping.

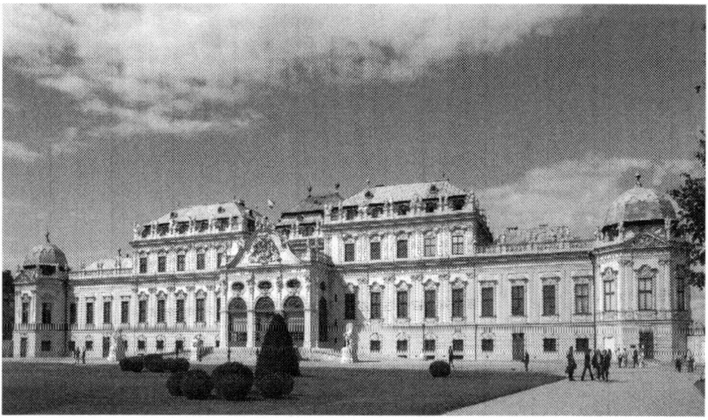

The Upper Belvedere

Here, we will explore the history, architecture, and art collections of Belvedere Palace, offering a detailed guide on what to see during your visit and an exploration of the surrounding area. We'll trace the story of Prince Eugene of Savoy, the great military leader for whom the palace was built, and discover the artistic treasures housed within this Baroque masterpiece.

Historical Overview: The Belvedere Palace was commissioned in the early 18th century by Prince Eugene of Savoy, one of Austria's greatest military commanders and a key figure in the Habsburg Empire's rise to power.

Born in Paris in 1663, Eugene initially sought a career in the French military but was rejected by Louis XIV due to his perceived lack of physical strength and aristocratic connections.

He moved to Austria and soon proved himself as a brilliant military strategist, playing a decisive role in the Great Turkish War and leading the Habsburg forces to victory at the Battle of Zenta (1697) and the Siege of Belgrade (1717).

As a reward for his military successes, Prince Eugene was granted vast estates and wealth, which allowed him to pursue his passion for art, architecture, and culture. He became one of the most important patrons of the arts in Austria, and the Belvedere Palace was designed as both a reflection of his wealth and a statement of his status within the Habsburg court.

The palace complex was designed by Johann Lukas von Hildebrandt, one of the leading Baroque architects of the time. Construction of the Lower Belvedere began in 1712, followed by the Upper Belvedere in 1721.

The two palaces were intended to complement each other: the Lower Belvedere served as Prince Eugene's residence, while the more formal Upper Belvedere was used for state functions and to house his extensive art collection.

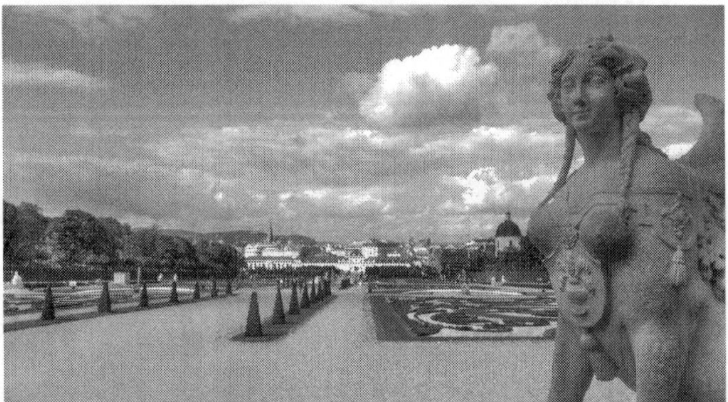

The view from the Upper Belvedere terrace, looking out over the garden towards the distant Lower Belvedere Palace.

After Prince Eugene's death in 1736, the palace became the property of the Habsburgs, and over time, it was transformed into a public museum, showcasing Austrian art and culture.

Architectural Highlights: The Belvedere Palace is a masterpiece of Baroque architecture, characterized by its grandeur, symmetry, and ornamental richness. Both the Upper and Lower Belvedere exhibit the typical elements of Baroque design: dramatic facades, elaborate decoration, and a strong sense of movement and dynamism, achieved through the use of curves, columns, and sculptural elements.

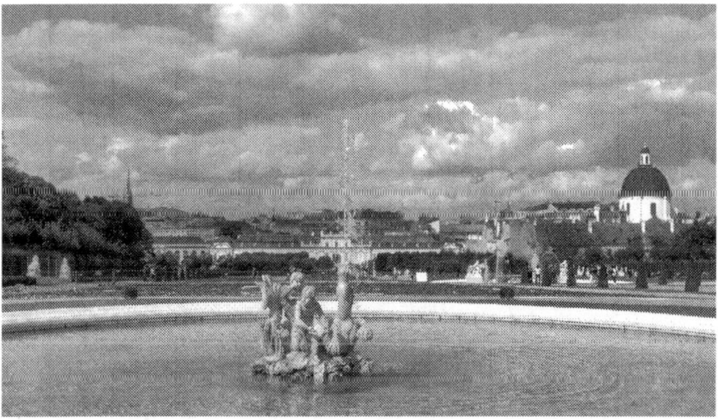

The Belvedere Gardens

Key architectural features include:

The Upper Belvedere: The grandest of the two palaces, the Upper Belvedere is a striking example of Baroque architecture. Its monumental façade features a central pavilion with an intricately decorated roof and a series of arched windows that allow light to flood into the interior. The pavilion is flanked by lower wings, creating a sense of balance and harmony. The entrance is adorned with statues of classical gods and goddesses, symbolizing the military victories of Prince Eugene. The grand staircase inside is one of the architectural highlights, with its sweeping curves and dramatic use of space.

The Lower Belvedere: The Lower Belvedere was designed as Prince Eugene's private residence and has a more intimate, domestic feel than the Upper Belvedere. Its façade is less imposing but still richly decorated with stucco work, sculptures, and reliefs. Inside, the Marble Hall and Gold Cabinet are particularly notable for their ornate design and luxurious use of materials.

The Orangery and Palace Stables, adjacent to the Lower Belvedere, were used to house Prince Eugene's extensive collection of exotic plants and horses, reflecting his wealth and refined tastes.

The Gardens: The formal gardens that connect the Upper and Lower Belvedere are designed in the French style, with geometric patterns, parterres, fountains, and carefully manicured lawns.

The gardens are arranged in three terraces, which descend from the Upper Belvedere to the Lower Belvedere, creating a sense of perspective and grandeur. The central axis of the gardens, aligned with the main entrance to the Upper Belvedere, is lined with statues of mythological figures, including Apollo, Venus, and Hercules, adding a sense of classical splendor to the landscape.

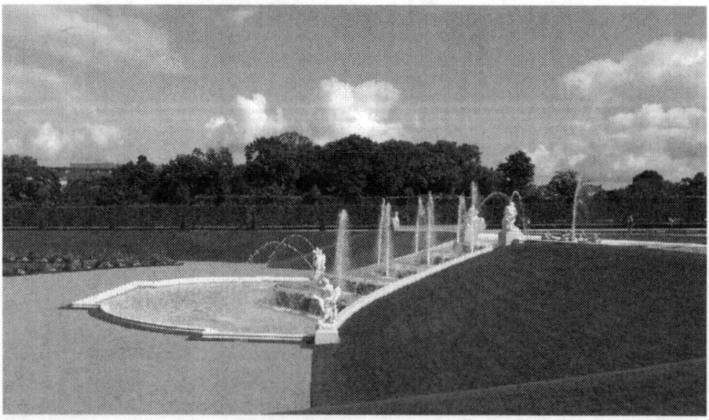

The Belvedere Gardens

Curiosity: Prince Eugene was known for his love of exotic animals, and the gardens once contained an aviary filled with rare birds and a menagerie of animals, including lions, tigers, and elephants.

This exotic display of wealth and power was intended to impress visitors and reinforce his status as one of the most powerful men in Europe.

What to See: A Step-by-Step Guide

Visiting the Belvedere Palace is a journey through the history of Austrian art, from the Middle Ages to the 20th century. The museum's collection is particularly strong in works from the Vienna Secession and Austrian Expressionism, with masterpieces by Gustav Klimt, Egon Schiele, and Oskar Kokoschka.

Here's a suggested itinerary that will take you through the highlights of both the Upper and Lower Belvedere, ensuring that you don't miss any of the palace's most important treasures.

The Upper Belvedere

Estimated time: 1.5-2 hours

Belvedere Museum | Belvedere Museum

Address: Prinz Eugen-Straße 27, 1030 Vienna

Public transport: Tram D to Schloss Belvedere

Opening hours: Daily: 10 a.m. – 6 p.m.

Online: www.belvedere.at/en/visit/upper-belvedere

Start your visit at the Upper Belvedere, where you will find the museum's most famous artworks, including Gustav Klimt's The Kiss.

The grand halls and state rooms of the palace provide an opulent setting for these masterpieces, offering visitors a unique experience of art within the context of Baroque architecture.

Key highlights include:

Gustav Klimt's The Kiss: Klimt's The Kiss (1907-1908) is one of the most famous paintings in the world and the highlight of the Belvedere's collection. This iconic work, which depicts two lovers embracing in a golden field of flowers, is a masterpiece of Symbolism and Art Nouveau. Klimt's use of gold leaf, intricate patterns, and sensual imagery has made the painting a symbol of love, beauty, and the artistic innovation of Vienna's Golden Age.

Other Works by Klimt: In addition to The Kiss, the Belvedere houses several other important works by Klimt, including Judith (1901), a provocative portrait of the biblical heroine, and Portrait of Fritza Riedler (1906), a striking example of Klimt's approach to portraiture.

Egon Schiele: The Belvedere also has an extensive collection of works by Egon Schiele, one of the most influential figures in Austrian Expressionism. Schiele's paintings, known for their raw emotional intensity and often distorted, angular figures, offer a stark contrast to Klimt's more decorative style. Highlights include The Embrace (1917) and Death and the Maiden (1915), both of which explore themes of love, death, and human vulnerability.

Oskar Kokoschka: Another key figure in Austrian modernism, Oskar Kokoschka is represented by several works in the Belvedere's collection. His expressive use of color and bold brushwork can be seen in paintings such as The Bride of the Wind (1914), which depicts Kokoschka's tumultuous relationship with composer Alma Mahler.

Medieval and Baroque Art: The Upper Belvedere's collection is not limited to modern art. It also includes significant works from earlier periods, such as medieval religious paintings, altarpieces, and Baroque portraits. Notable pieces include the Adoration of the Magi by Hieronymus Bosch, as well as portraits of the Habsburg rulers by Johann Peter Krafft and Franz Anton Maulbertsch.

Curiosity:: Prince Eugene's private collection of paintings, which once hung in the Upper Belvedere, included masterpieces by Titian, Caravaggio, and Peter Paul Rubens. These works were later transferred to the Kunsthistorisches Museum but left a lasting legacy on the palace's role as a center of art and culture.

The Gardens

Estimated time: 30-45 minutes

After exploring the Upper Belvedere, take a stroll through the formal gardens that connect the two palaces. The gardens are designed in the French style, with symmetrical layouts, geometric flowerbeds, and ornamental fountains. The gardens are arranged on three terraces, which descend from the Upper Belvedere to the Lower Belvedere, offering sweeping views of the city skyline and the palace itself.

As you walk through the gardens, take note of the classical statues and sculptures that line the pathways. These figures, representing gods, goddesses, and mythological heroes, add a sense of grandeur and elegance to the landscape. The central axis of the gardens is particularly impressive, with a long reflecting pool that creates a mirror-like surface, reflecting the façade of the Upper Belvedere.

Curiosity: The gardens were originally designed as a space for formal receptions and outdoor entertainment. During Prince Eugene's time, the gardens hosted grand balls, banquets, and performances, making them an integral part of the palace's social and cultural life.

The Lower Belvedere

Estimated time: 1-1.5 hours

Next, head to the Lower Belvedere, which was originally built as Prince Eugene's private residence.

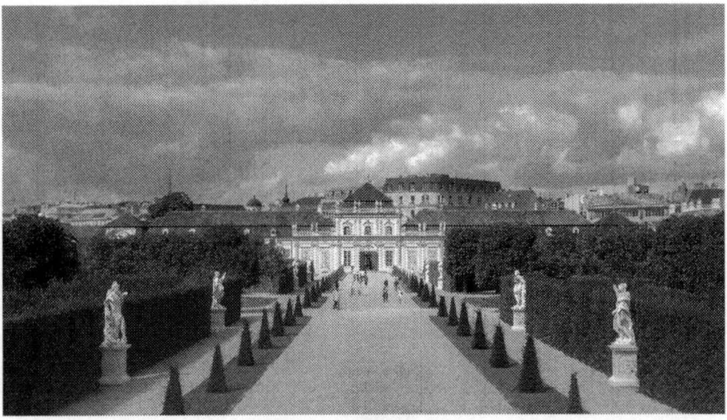

The Lower Belvedere

While smaller and more intimate than the Upper Belvedere, the Lower Belvedere is equally rich in architectural and artistic treasures. The interior rooms are lavishly decorated, with ornate stucco ceilings, marble floors, and gilded furnishings.

Key highlights include:

The Marble Hall: The grand Marble Hall is one of the most opulent rooms in the Lower Belvedere. This double-height room is adorned with marble columns, a frescoed ceiling, and large windows that flood the space with natural light. The hall was used for formal receptions and state functions, and its design reflects the grandeur of Prince Eugene's court.

The Gold Cabinet: The Gold Cabinet is a small, richly decorated room that once served as Prince Eugene's private study. The walls are covered in gilded wood paneling, and the ceiling features an elaborate stucco design. The room's intimate scale and luxurious decoration make it one of the most charming spaces in the palace.

Temporary Exhibitions: The Lower Belvedere also hosts temporary exhibitions, which showcase works from the museum's collection, as well as loans from other institutions. These exhibitions often focus on specific artists, movements, or themes, offering visitors a deeper understanding of Austrian art and culture.

The Orangery and Palace Stables: Adjacent to the Lower Belvedere are the Orangery and Palace Stables, which were originally used to house Prince Eugene's collection of exotic plants and horses. Today, these spaces are used for temporary exhibitions and special events. The Orangery, with its large windows and elegant proportions, is particularly beautiful in the spring and summer when the surrounding gardens are in full bloom.

Curiosity: Prince Eugene was a passionate collector of plants, and the Orangery was designed to house his collection of citrus trees, rare flowers, and tropical plants. The building was heated by a system of underground furnaces, allowing the plants to thrive even in the cold Viennese winters.

Exploring the Surrounding Area

The Belvedere Palace is located in the Rennweg district, a short distance from Vienna's city center. The area surrounding the palace is rich in history and culture, with several other important landmarks and attractions nearby.

Schwarzenbergplatz

Location: 1 kilometer / 0.62 miles from the Lower Belvedere

Walking time: 10-12 minutes

Schwarzenbergplatz is a grand square located just a short walk from the Belvedere Palace. The square is dominated by the Equestrian Statue of Prince Karl Philipp of Schwarzenberg, another famous Austrian military commander. The square is also home to the Soviet War Memorial, which commemorates the soldiers who liberated Vienna during WW II.

The Vienna Konzerthaus

Location: 1.5 kilometers / 0.93 miles from the Lower Belvedere

Walking time: 18-20 minutes

For music lovers, a visit to the Vienna Konzerthaus is a must. Located just a short distance from the Belvedere Palace, the Konzerthaus is one of Vienna's most important concert halls and hosts performances by the Vienna Symphony Orchestra, as well as international artists and ensembles.

The building, completed in 1913, is a beautiful example of Jugendstil (Art Nouveau) architecture and features several performance spaces, including the grand Great Hall.

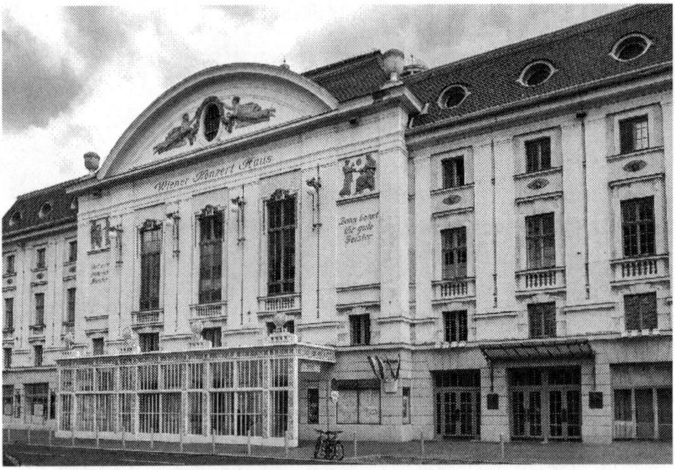

The Vienna Konzerthaus

Wiener Konzerthaus | The Vienna Konzerthaus

Address: Lothringerstraße 20, 1030 Vienna

Public transport: U4 to Stadtpark

Opening hours: Depends on events

Online: www.konzerthaus.at

MuseumsQuartier

Location: Museumsplatz 1, 1070 Vienna

Public transport: Tram D from Schloss Belvedere to Karlsplatz, then U2 to MuseumsQuartier

Walking distance: Approximately 2.4 kilometers / 1.5 miles

Walking time: Around 30-35 minutes

After exploring the Belvedere Palace, head to the MuseumsQuartier, one of the largest cultural complexes in the world. It houses a variety of institutions, including the Leopold Museum, known for its extensive Egon Schiele collection, and MUMOK, dedicated to modern art. This dynamic hub blends contemporary art with historic architecture, offering visitors exhibitions, performances, and relaxing courtyards.

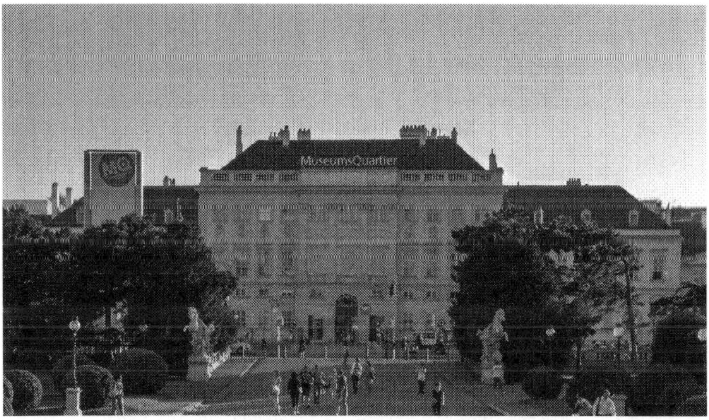

The MuseumsQuartier (MQ)

Curiosity: The brightly colored modular outdoor seats, known as Enzis, have become an iconic feature of the MuseumsQuartier courtyards, offering a unique spot to relax amidst the cultural surroundings.

The MuseumsQuartier (MQ) is one of the largest cultural complexes in the world, blending historic architecture with modern, innovative design to create a vibrant center for art, culture, and leisure. Located in the heart of Vienna, near the Ringstrasse and just a stone's throw from the city's most famous museums and historic sites, the MuseumsQuartier is home to a wide range of museums, galleries, performance spaces, and cultural institutions. It encompasses everything from contemporary art and architecture to dance, music, theater, and multimedia exhibitions.

Occupying the former imperial stables of the Habsburgs, the MQ is a prime example of how Vienna successfully merges its rich imperial past with modern cultural innovation. Opened in 2001, this vast cultural district covers over 90,000 square meters (970,000 square feet) and houses institutions such as the Leopold Museum, the Museum of Modern Art Ludwig Foundation (MUMOK), the Kunsthalle Wien, the Architecture Center Vienna (Az W), and more. The MQ has become a dynamic cultural space where visitors can explore the cutting edge of the contemporary art scene, enjoy outdoor festivals, and relax in its stylish courtyards.

We'll explore the historical and architectural significance of the MuseumsQuartier, examine its major museums and institutions, and provide a detailed guide on what to see during your visit. We'll also look at how the MQ interacts with the surrounding cultural landmarks, making it one of Vienna's most popular and dynamic destinations.

Historical Overview: The history of the MuseumsQuartier dates back to the early 18th century when the area was developed as part of the Hofburg Palace complex. The buildings that now make up the MQ were originally constructed as the imperial stables for the Habsburg court. Designed by Johann Bernhard Fischer von Erlach, the stables were built in the Baroque style, reflecting the grandeur and opulence of the Habsburg monarchy.

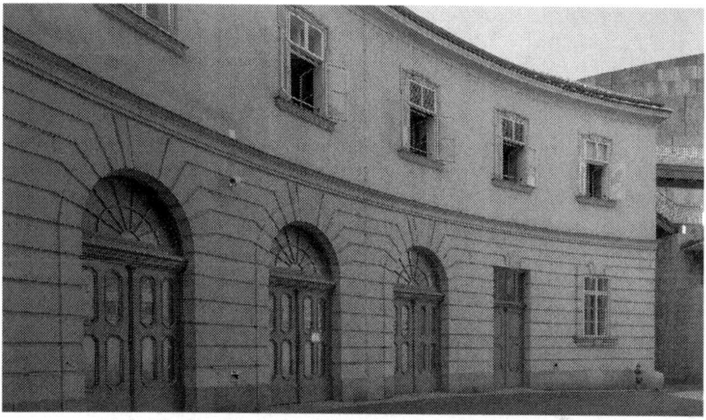

The former Imperial Stables of the Vienna court.

The stables housed the horses and carriages of the imperial family and were part of a larger complex that included the nearby Hofburg Palace, the Spanish Riding School, and other imperial institutions. Over the centuries, the area was expanded and modified, but by the late 20th century, the stables had fallen into disuse, and the city of Vienna began looking for new ways to repurpose the space.

In the 1990s, the decision was made to transform the site into a major cultural district, combining the historic Baroque architecture with bold, contemporary design. The result was the MuseumsQuartier, a modern cultural center that opened to the public in 2001. Today, the MQ is not only one of the largest cultural complexes in Europe but also a symbol of Vienna's ability to embrace both its imperial heritage and its role as a leading center for contemporary art and culture.

Architectural Significance: One of the most striking aspects of the MuseumsQuartier is the way it blends historic architecture with modern design. The original Baroque stables have been preserved and renovated, while new, cutting-edge buildings have been added to create a dynamic contrast between old and new. The interplay between the two architectural styles is a defining feature of the MQ and reflects

Vienna's broader approach to urban development, where the city's imperial past coexists with its contemporary cultural ambitions.

Key architectural features include:

The Baroque Facades: The original buildings, designed by Fischer von Erlach, are a fine example of Baroque architecture, with their grand facades, symmetrical layouts, and ornate details. These structures have been carefully restored and now house institutions such as the Leopold Museum and the Architekturzentrum Wien. The Baroque facades create a sense of continuity with Vienna's historic city center, linking the MuseumsQuartier to the surrounding Ringstrasse buildings.

Contemporary Additions: The most notable contemporary additions to the MQ include the Museum of Modern Art Ludwig Foundation (MUMOK) and the Kunsthalle Wien. Both buildings are stark, minimalist structures that contrast sharply with the surrounding Baroque architecture. The MUMOK, designed by Ortner & Ortner, is a monolithic gray basalt cube that looms over the central courtyard, while the Kunsthalle is a sleek glass and steel pavilion that houses temporary exhibitions of cutting-edge contemporary art.

The Main Courtyards: The MuseumsQuartier is centered around two large courtyards: the Haupthof (Main Courtyard) and the Hof 2 (Second Courtyard). These open-air spaces are designed for public gatherings, outdoor exhibitions, performances, and relaxation. The courtyards are furnished with brightly colored, modular seating known as Enzis, which have become iconic features of the MQ. The contrast between the Baroque buildings and the modern courtyard furniture reflects the MQ's unique blend of tradition and innovation.

Curiosity: The bright and colorful Enzis, designed by Viennese architects PPAG, have become one of the most recognizable symbols of the MuseumsQuartier. These modular outdoor seats are moved around the courtyards depending on the season, offering visitors a place to relax and socialize in a playful and dynamic environment.

What to See: A Step-by-Step Guide

The MuseumsQuartier is home to a wide variety of museums and cultural institutions, each offering a unique perspective on art, architecture, and contemporary culture. Here is a step-by-step guide to exploring the key highlights of the MQ, ensuring that you make the most of your visit.

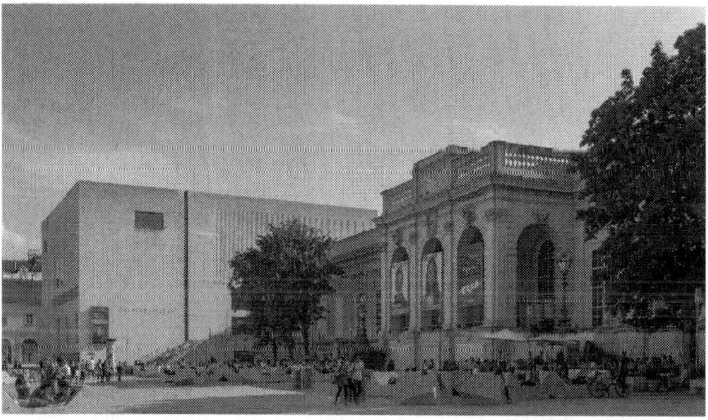

The Leopold Museum (left) and the Kunsthale (right)

Leopold Museum

Estimated time: 1-1.5 hours

The Leopold Museum is one of the most important cultural institutions in Vienna, housing the world's largest collection of works by Egon Schiele, as well as masterpieces by Gustav Klimt, Oskar Kokoschka, and other key figures of Austrian modernism.

The museum was founded by art collectors Rudolf and Elisabeth Leopold, whose private collection forms the basis of the museum's holdings.

Key highlights include:

Egon Schiele: The Leopold Museum holds over 200 works by Egon Schiele, including some of his most famous paintings and drawings. Schiele's intense, often unsettling portraits and self-portraits explore themes of isolation, sexuality, and existential angst. Notable works include "Self-Portrait with Physalis" (1912) and "Death and the Maiden" (1915), both of which exemplify Schiele's raw, expressive style.

Gustav Klimt: The museum also features several important works by Gustav Klimt, including his early landscapes and portraits. One of the highlights is Klimt's "Death and Life" (1910-1915), a large, symbolic painting that reflects Klimt's fascination with the cycle of life and death.

Vienna 1900: The Leopold Museum offers a comprehensive look at the Vienna Secession and the Vienna 1900 movement, which saw artists like Schiele and Klimt breaking away from academic traditions to explore new forms of artistic expression.

The museum's collection includes furniture, decorative arts, and design objects from this period, offering a broader understanding of the cultural and intellectual climate of Fin de Siècle Vienna.

Leopold Museum | Leopold Museum

Address: Museumsplatz 1, 1070 Vienna

Public transport: U2 to Museumsquartier

Opening hours: Mon, Wed-Sun: 10 a.m. – 6 p.m.; Thu: 10 a.m. – 9 p.m.; Tue: closed

Online: www.leopoldmuseum.org/en

Museum of Modern Art Ludwig Foundation (MUMOK)

Estimated time: 1-1.5 hours

The MUMOK (Museum Moderner Kunst Stiftung Ludwig Wien) is the largest museum of modern and contemporary art in Central Europe, with a collection that spans the 20th and 21st centuries. The museum's focus is on avant-garde and experimental art, with works by artists from movements such as Cubism, Surrealism, Pop Art, and Conceptual Art.

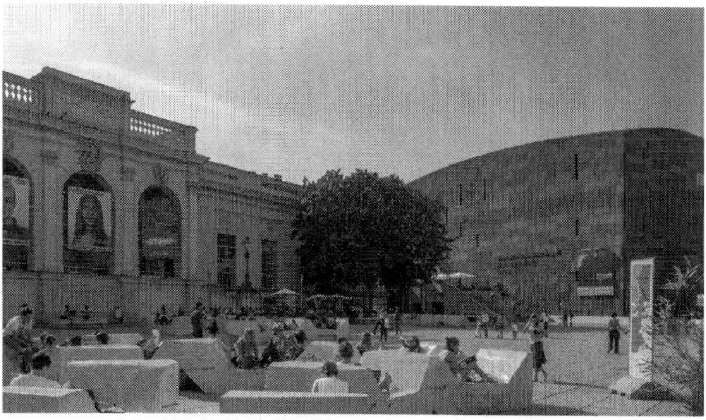

The Kunsthale (left) and the MUMOK (right)

Key highlights include:

Pop Art and Fluxus: MUMOK's collection features important works from the Pop Art movement, including pieces by Andy Warhol, Roy Lichtenstein, and Claes Oldenburg. The museum also houses works by Fluxus artists, who challenged traditional notions of art through performances, happenings, and multimedia installations.

Viennese Actionism: One of the museum's most significant holdings is its collection of works by the Viennese Actionists, a group of radical artists who used performance art to explore themes of violence, sexuality, and the human body. The group, which included artists such as Günter Brus and Rudolf Schwarzkogler, pushed the boundaries of what was considered acceptable in art, often courting controversy and scandal.

Contemporary Installations: In addition to its permanent collection, MUMOK regularly hosts temporary exhibitions that showcase the latest trends in contemporary art. These exhibitions often feature large-scale installations, video art, and immersive multimedia experiences that challenge visitors to think critically about the role of art in contemporary society.

Curiosity: MUMOK's building, a stark, gray basalt

cube, was designed by architects Ortner & Ortner to reflect the museum's focus on contemporary art. Its minimalist, industrial appearance contrasts sharply with the Baroque architecture of the surrounding MuseumsQuartier, making it a visual symbol of the museum's avant-garde mission.

MUMOK | MUMOK

Address: Museumsplatz 1, 1070 Vienna

Public transport: U2 to Museumsquartier

Opening hours: Mon, Wed-Sun: 10 a.m. – 6 p.m.; Thu: 10 a.m. – 9 p.m.; Tue: closed

Online: www.mumok.at/en/

Kunsthalle Wien

Estimated time: 45 minutes - 1 hour

The Kunsthalle Wien is Vienna's leading space for contemporary art exhibitions, featuring rotating shows that highlight cutting-edge artists from around the world. Unlike the Leopold Museum and MUMOK, the Kunsthalle does not have a permanent collection, allowing it to focus entirely on temporary exhibitions that explore current trends in visual art, photography, video, and performance.

The Kunsthalle is known for its experimental approach to curating, often showcasing works that challenge traditional boundaries between art, politics, and society. Past exhibitions have explored themes such as globalization, migration, digital culture, and the environment, making the Kunsthalle a space for dialogue and reflection on contemporary issues.

Curiosity: The Kunsthalle's location within the MuseumsQuartier, combined with its focus on contemporary art, makes it a dynamic and ever-changing institution. Its exhibitions often engage with the broader cultural landscape of Vienna, connecting local and international artistic communities.

Kunsthalle Wien | Kunsthalle Vienna

Address: Museumsplatz 1, 1070 Vienna

Public transport: U2 to Museumsquartier

Opening hours: Daily: 10:00 – 19:00

Online: https://kunsthallewien.at/en/

Vienna State Opera

Location: Opernring 2, 1010 Vienna

Public transport: U2 from MuseumsQuartier to Karlsplatz

Walking distance: Approximately 900 meters / 0.56 miles

Walking time: Around 10-12 minutes

Wiener Staatsoper | Vienna State Opera

Address: Opernring 2, 1010 Vienna

Public transport: U1, U2, U4 to Karlsplatz

Opening hours: Performance times vary

Online: www.wiener-staatsoper.at/en/

After your visit to the MuseumsQuartier, head to the Vienna State Opera, a world-renowned Neo-Renaissance masterpiece designed by August Sicard von Sicardsburg and Eduard van der Nüll. Opened in 1869 with a performance of Mozart's Don Giovanni, it remains one of the leading opera houses globally, hosting more than 350 performances each year.

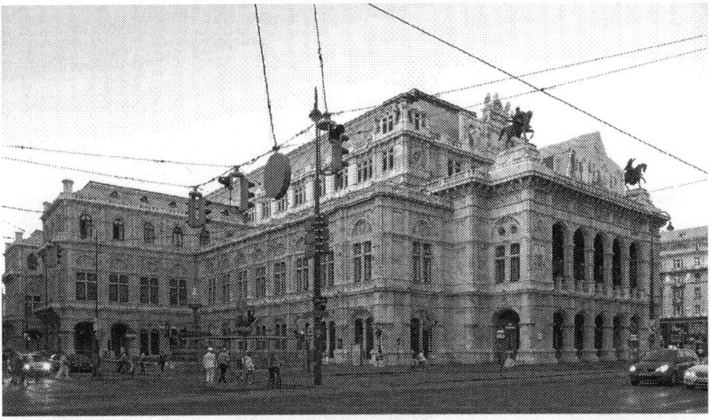

Vienna State Opera

Curiosity: *The Vienna Opera Ball*, held annually in this magnificent venue, transforms the auditorium into a glamorous ballroom, attended by Vienna's high society and celebrities from around the world.

The Vienna State Opera (Wiener Staatsoper) is one of the most prestigious and renowned opera houses in the world, a symbol of Vienna's deep connection to music and culture. Since its opening in 1869, the Vienna State Opera has been at the heart of Austria's musical life, hosting performances by some of the greatest composers, conductors, and singers in history. The grand building, located on the famous Ringstrasse, is an architectural masterpiece and one of the most recognizable landmarks in Vienna.

Historical Overview: The Vienna State Opera was born during a period of great cultural and architectural expansion in Vienna. In the mid-19th century, Emperor Franz Joseph I ordered the construction of the Ringstrasse, a grand boulevard encircling the city's historic center. The Ringstrasse was lined with monumental buildings, including the Kunsthistorisches Museum, the Naturhistorisches Museum, the Austrian Parliament, and the Rathaus (City Hall). Among these was the Vienna State Opera, designed to be the city's premier venue for opera and ballet performances.

Construction of the opera house began in 1861 under the direction of architects Eduard van der Nüll and August Sicard von Sicardsburg, both of whom were prominent figures in Austrian architecture at the time. The building was designed in the Neo-Renaissance style, reflecting the ideals of the Renaissance revival that emphasized classical symmetry, proportion, and decorative detail. The opera house was completed in 1869, and its inaugural performance was Mozart's Don Giovanni, chosen to honor Vienna's most famous composer.

Despite its importance, the Vienna State Opera's opening was overshadowed by controversy. Many critics were disappointed with the building's design, which they considered too modest and lacking in grandeur compared to other structures on the Ringstrasse. The building's position, slightly below street level due to the construction of the Ringstrasse, earned it the unflattering nickname "the sunken treasure chest". Tragically, both van der Nüll and Sicardsburg died before the opera house was completed—van der Nüll by suicide, reportedly due to the harsh criticism, and Sicardsburg from illness just weeks later.

However, over time, the Vienna State Opera became a beloved institution, and its design was eventually recognized for its elegance and harmony with the surrounding cityscape.

Exploring the Surrounding Area

The Vienna State Opera is located in the heart of Vienna's Innere Stadt, making it a perfect starting point for exploring some of the city's most famous landmarks and cultural institutions.

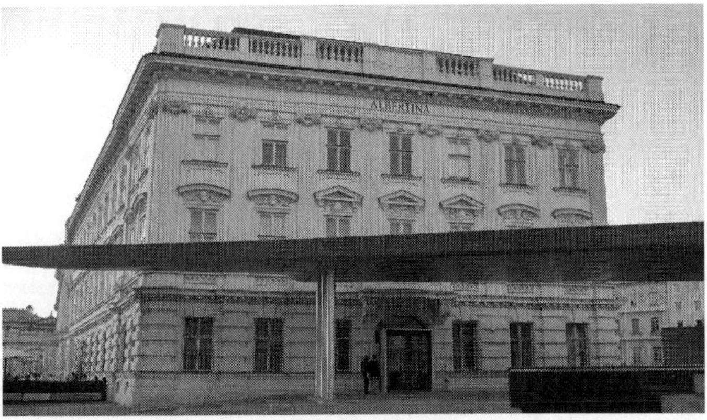

The Albertina Museum

Albertina Museum

Location: 300 meters / 0.19 miles from the Vienna State Opera

Walking time: 5 minutes

Just a short walk from the Vienna State Opera is the Albertina Museum, one of Vienna's premier art museums. The Albertina is home to one of the most important collections of graphic art in the world, with works by artists such as Albrecht Dürer, Rembrandt, and Michelangelo. The museum also features rotating exhibitions of modern and contemporary art, including works by Pablo Picasso, Monet, and Edvard Munch.

Curiosity: The Albertina's Habsburg Staterooms offer a glimpse into the imperial past of the building, with lavishly decorated rooms that once housed members of the Habsburg family.

Albertina Museum | Albertina Museum

Address: Albertinaplatz 1, 1010 Vienna

Public transport: U1 to Stephansplatz

Opening hours: Daily: 10 a.m. – 6 p.m.

Online: www.albertina.at/en/

Hotel Sacher

Location: 100 meters / 0.06 miles from the Vienna State Opera

Walking time: 2 minutes

Directly across from the Vienna State Opera is the famous Hotel Sacher, home to the original Sachertorte, a rich chocolate cake filled with apricot jam. The hotel's Café Sacher is a must-visit for anyone with a sweet tooth, offering not only the legendary cake but also a selection of traditional Viennese pastries and coffee.

Curiosity: The Sachertorte was invented by Franz Sacher in 1832 for Prince Metternich, and it has since become one of Austria's most famous desserts.

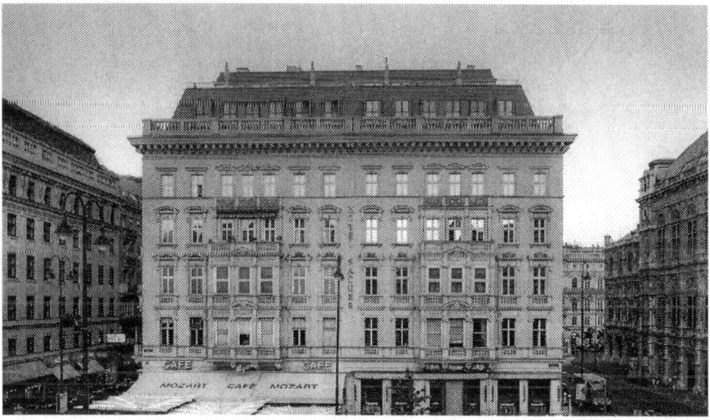

Hotel Sacher

Hotel Sacher | Hotel Sacher

Address: Philharmonikerstraße 4, 1010 Vienna

Public transport: U1, U2, U4 to Karlsplatz

Online: www.sacher.com/en/

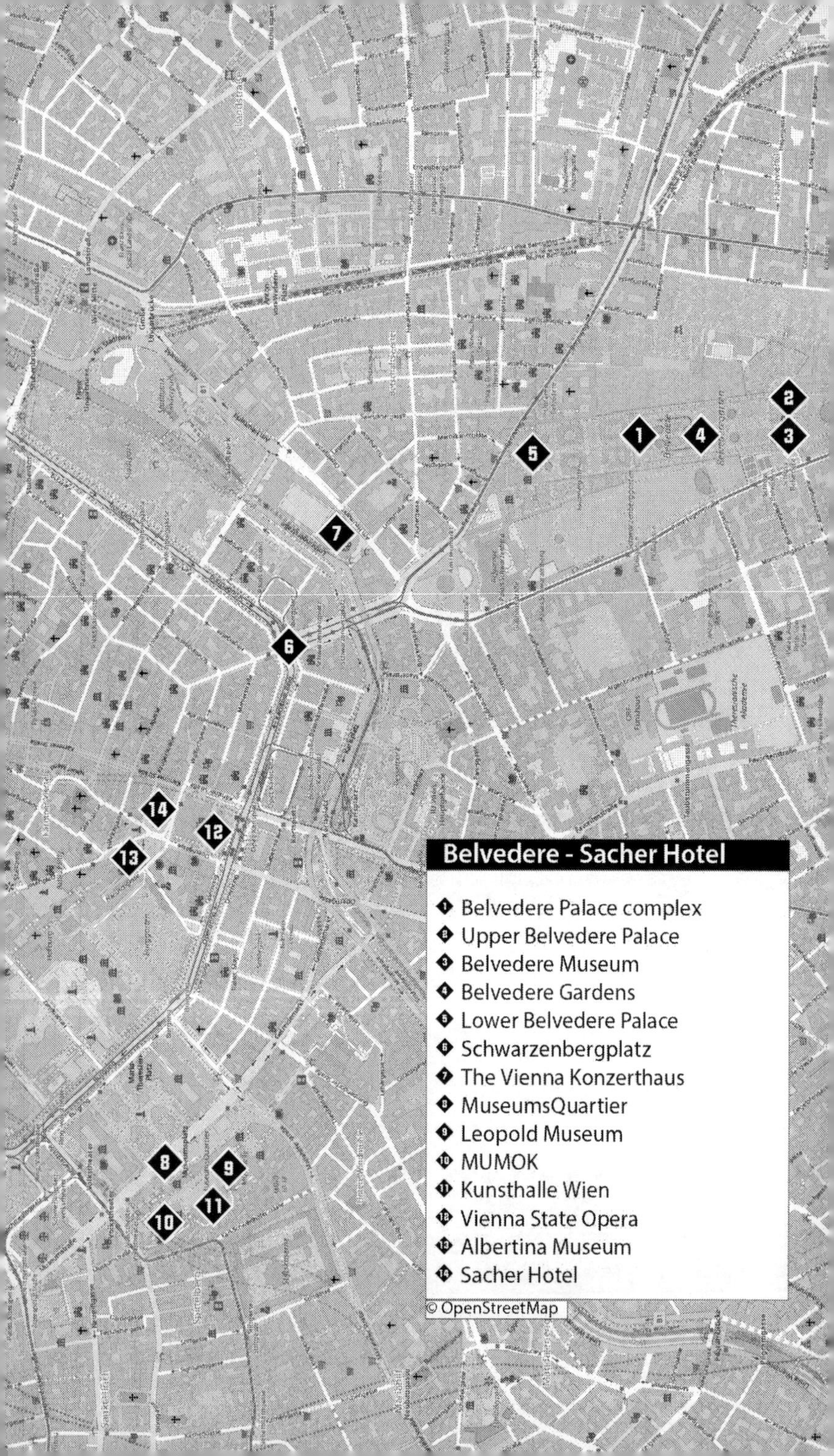

Belvedere - Sacher Hotel
1 Belvedere Palace complex
2 Upper Belvedere Palace
3 Belvedere Museum
4 Belvedere Gardens
5 Lower Belvedere Palace
6 Schwarzenbergplatz
7 The Vienna Konzerthaus
8 MuseumsQuartier
9 Leopold Museum
10 MUMOK
11 Kunsthalle Wien
12 Vienna State Opera
13 Albertina Museum
14 Sacher Hotel
© OpenStreetMap

SCHÖNBRUNN WALK – BAROQUE SPLENDOR

Schönbrunn Palace complex

Walking distance from Old Town: Approximately 4 kilometers / 2.5 miles

Walking time: Around 50-55 minutes

Schloss Schönbrunn | Schönbrunn Palace

Address: Schönbrunner Schloßstraße 47, 1130 Vienna

Public transport: U4 to Schönbrunn or Hiezing Station

Opening hours: Daily: 9 a.m. – 5 p.m.

Online: www.schoenbrunn.at/en/

After visiting the MuseumsQuartier, head to Schönbrunn Palace, one of Vienna's most iconic Baroque palaces, designed by Johann Bernhard Fischer von Erlach.

Once the summer residence of the Habsburgs, this UNESCO World Heritage site is known for its ornate state rooms, vast gardens, and the world's oldest zoo. Highlights include the Great Gallery,

Empress Maria Theresa's apartments, and the Gloriette, which offers panoramic views of the city.

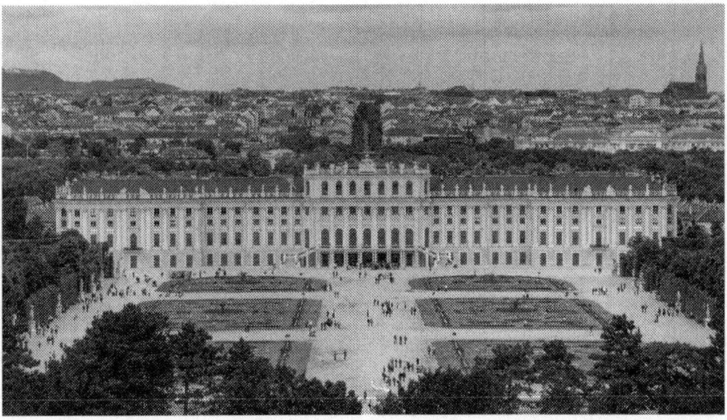

The Schönbrunn Palace

Curiosity: The palace gardens also feature a unique Maze and a Palm House, which showcases a wide range of exotic plants in one of the largest greenhouses in Europe.

Schönbrunn Palace (Schloss Schönbrunn) is one of the most significant cultural monuments in Austria and one of Europe's most impressive Baroque palaces. Located in the western part of Vienna, Schönbrunn was the summer residence of the Habsburg dynasty, rulers of Austria and one of the most powerful royal families in European history. The palace, with its vast gardens, majestic architecture, and stunning interiors, reflects the splendor and wealth of the Habsburgs and their desire to create a residence that could rival the grandest palaces in Europe, including Versailles.

Today, Schönbrunn Palace is a UNESCO World Heritage Site and one of Austria's most visited attractions. It offers visitors a chance to step back in time and explore the opulent lifestyle of the Habsburg monarchs, particularly during the reign of Empress Maria Theresa and Emperor Franz Joseph I. The palace complex includes more than just the grand Baroque residence—it features beautifully landscaped gardens, fountains, statues, the Gloriette (a hilltop pavilion with panoramic views), and the world's oldest zoo.

W will explore the history, architecture, and cultural significance of Schönbrunn Palace, providing a comprehensive guide on what to see during your visit. We'll also delve into the surrounding area, including the magnificent gardens, the Schönbrunn Zoo, and other nearby attractions that enhance the visitor experience.

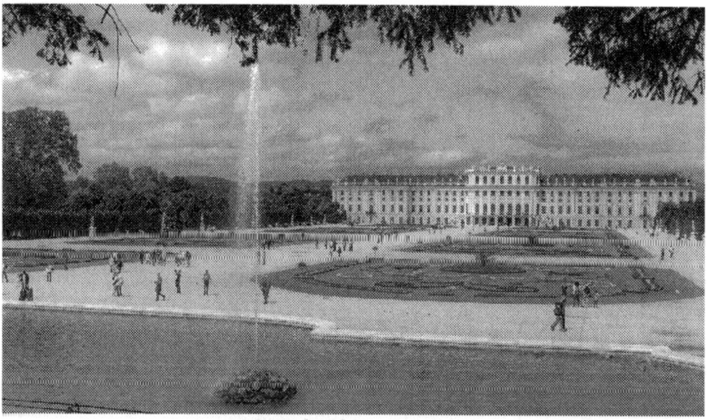

The Schönbrunn Palace

Historical Overview: The history of Schönbrunn Palace dates back to the late 16th century, when the area was used as a hunting ground by the Habsburgs. The name "Schönbrunn" (meaning "beautiful spring") is derived from an artesian well located on the site. In 1642, Eleonora Gonzaga, the wife of Emperor Ferdinand II, commissioned the construction of a small hunting lodge. However, it was Emperor Leopold I who, in the late 17th century, began transforming the site into a grand residence.

The palace we see today was largely shaped by the vision of Empress Maria Theresa, who ruled Austria from 1740 to 1780. Under her direction, Schönbrunn was transformed into a lavish summer residence for the imperial family. Maria Theresa's architect, Nicolaus Pacassi, redesigned the palace in the Baroque style, with extensive gardens and elaborate interiors. Schönbrunn became the center of court life during the reign of Maria Theresa, who entertained European royalty, diplomats, and artists within its opulent halls.

During the 19th century, Emperor Franz Joseph I, the longest-reigning emperor of Austria, spent much of his time at Schönbrunn. It was here that Franz Joseph was born in 1830, and it remained his favored residence throughout his reign. His wife, Empress Elisabeth, known as Sisi, also resided at the palace, although she famously disliked the formalities of court life.

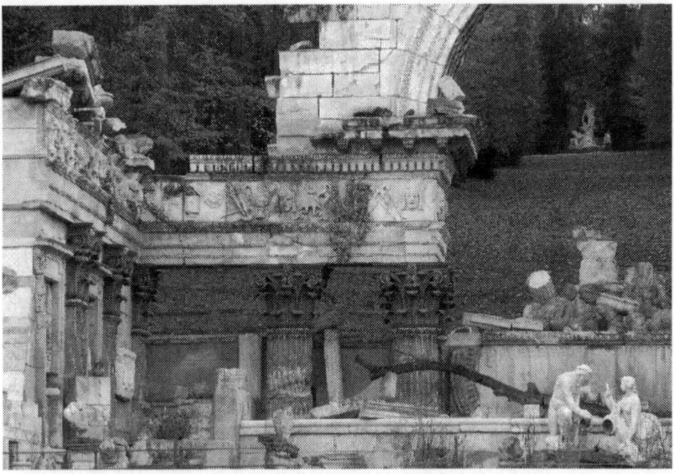

The Schönbrunn Gardens

After the fall of the Habsburg monarchy in 1918, following World War I, Schönbrunn became the property of the newly formed Republic of Austria. It was opened to the public and has since become one of the country's most important cultural and historical landmarks.

Architectural Highlights: Schönbrunn Palace is a masterpiece of Baroque architecture, designed to impress with its scale, symmetry, and grandeur. The palace consists of 1,441 rooms, although only a fraction of these are open to the public. The combination of majestic facades, elegant interiors, and beautifully landscaped gardens make Schönbrunn one of the most impressive royal residences in Europe.

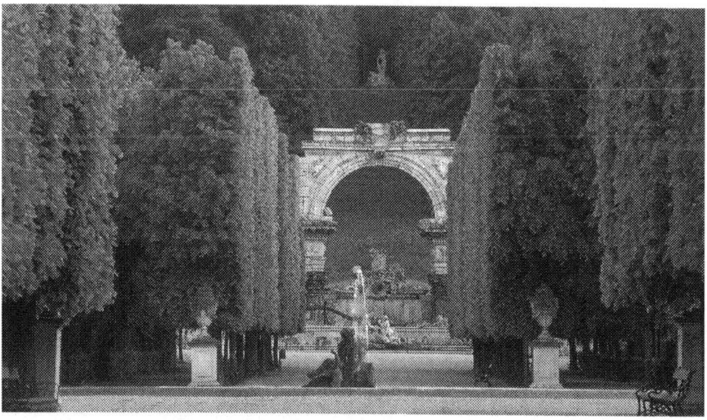

The Schönbrunn Gardens

Key architectural features include:

The Grand Facade: The palace's main facade is a stunning example of Baroque design, with its clean lines, symmetrical layout, and classical proportions. The soft yellow color of the palace, known as "Schönbrunn yellow", has become iconic and is now associated with the Habsburg monarchy. The facade is adorned with decorative elements, including balustrades, pediments, and sculpted reliefs, that reflect the grandeur of the imperial court.

The Great Gallery (Große Galerie): Inside, the Great Gallery is one of the most opulent rooms in the palace. This long, ceremonial hall is richly decorated with gilded stucco, crystal chandeliers, and ceiling frescoes by Gregorio Guglielmi that depict allegories of Habsburg virtues and victories.

The room was used for state banquets, balls, and grand receptions, and it remains one of the most breathtaking spaces in the palace.

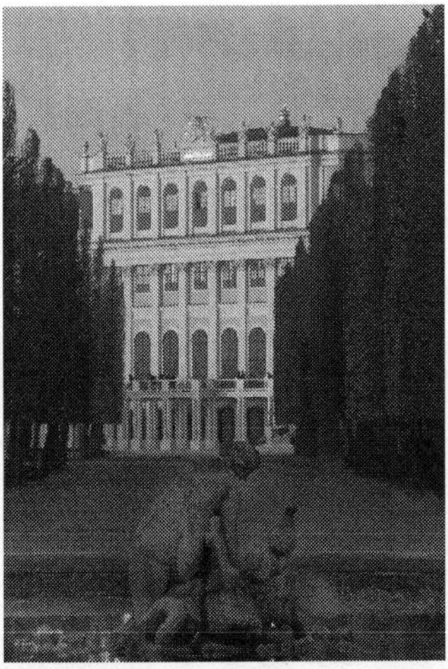
The Schönbrunn Palace

The Blue Chinese Salon and the Vieux-Laque Room: Schönbrunn is famous for its rooms decorated in Chinoiserie style, a European interpretation of Chinese and East Asian art. The Blue Chinese Salon and the Vieux-Laque Room are two of the most beautiful examples of this style in the palace, with walls adorned with delicate Chinese porcelain and lacquer panels. The Vieux-Laque Room, in particular, was a favorite of Empress Maria Theresa, and it was here that Emperor Charles I signed his abdication in 1918, marking the end of the Habsburg monarchy.

The Mirror Room: Another highlight is the Mirror Room, where the young Wolfgang Amadeus Mozart performed for Empress Maria Theresa at the age of six. The room is lined with large mirrors that reflect the light from the chandeliers, creating a dazzling effect that enhances the room's sense of grandeur.

The Imperial Apartments: The private apartments of Emperor Franz Joseph and Empress Elisabeth offer a glimpse into the everyday life of the imperial family. Franz Joseph's rooms are relatively modest, reflecting his simple lifestyle and dedication to work, while Sisi's apartments are more ornate, featuring luxurious furniture and personal items that reveal her love of beauty and fashion.

Curiosity: Schönbrunn's architectural design was influenced by the French Palace of Versailles, which served as a model for many European monarchs seeking to build grand residences that reflected their power and wealth. However, Schönbrunn's distinct yellow facade and Austrian Baroque style give it a unique identity.

What to See: A Step-by-Step Guide

Visiting Schönbrunn Palace is a comprehensive experience that takes visitors through the grandeur of Habsburg life, from the ornate state rooms to the tranquil gardens. Here is a step-by-step guide to exploring the palace and its many attractions.

The State Rooms and Imperial Apartments

Estimated time: 1.5-2 hours

Begin your visit with a tour of the State Rooms and Imperial Apartments, which offer a glimpse into the lives of the Habsburg rulers. The Grand Tour takes visitors through 40 rooms, while the shorter Imperial Tour covers 22 rooms. Either tour will allow you to experience the palace's most opulent spaces, including the Great Gallery, the Hall of Ceremonies, the Hall of Mirrors, and the private apartments of Emperor Franz Joseph and Empress Elisabeth.

Key highlights include:

The Great Gallery: This stunning ballroom, with its gilded stucco and frescoed ceiling, is the most impressive room in the palace. The room's grandeur is enhanced by its size—measuring 40 meters (131 feet) long and 10 meters (33 feet) wide—and the opulent decorations that adorn every surface.

The Blue Chinese Salon and the Vieux-Laque Room: These rooms showcase the Habsburgs' fascination with Asian art, featuring exquisite Chinese porcelain, lacquer panels, and Oriental-inspired decor. The Vieux-Laque Room is particularly important historically, as it was where the last Habsburg emperor, Charles I, signed his abdication in 1918.

Franz Joseph's and Sisi's Apartments: The personal living quarters of Franz Joseph and Sisi offer a more intimate glimpse into their lives. Franz Joseph's rooms are simple and functional, reflecting his disciplined character, while Sisi's rooms are more ornate, with richly decorated furniture and personal items that reflect her love of beauty and fitness.

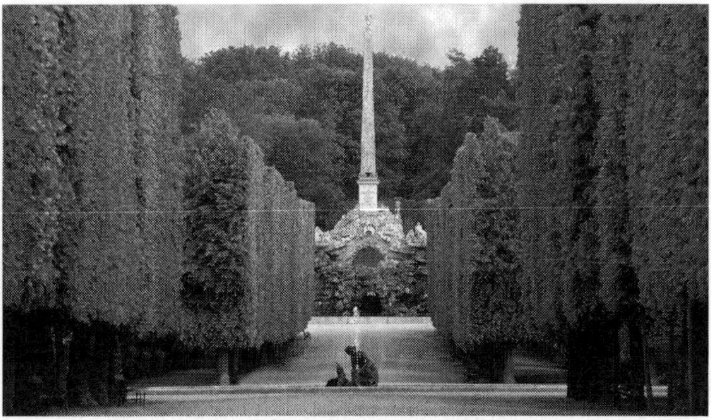

The Gardens and Fountains

Curiosity: Sisi, known for her beauty and her rebellious spirit, had a gymnasium installed in her apartments at Schönbrunn, which included rings and a balance beam—quite unusual for an empress of her time.

The Gardens and Fountains

Estimated time: 1-1.5 hours

The gardens cover an area of 1.2 square kilometers (300 acres) and are filled with fountains, statues, flowerbeds, and tree-lined avenues.

Key highlights include:

The Neptune Fountain: Located at the foot of the hill that leads to the Gloriette, the Neptune Fountain is one of the most impressive features of the gardens.

The fountain, completed in 1780, depicts the sea god Neptune surrounded by nymphs and tritons, symbolizing Habsburg power over land and sea.

Schönbrunner Gärten | Schönbrunn Gardens

Address: Schönbrunner Schloßstraße 47, 1130 Vienna

Public transport: U4 to Schönbrunn

Opening hours: Daily: 6:30 a.m. – 6 p.m.

Online: www.schoenbrunn.at/en/

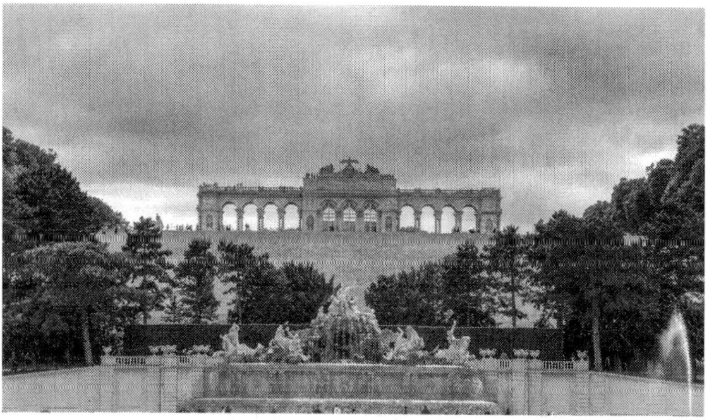

The Gloriette

The Gloriette: Perched on a hill overlooking the palace, the Gloriette is a grand pavilion that offers panoramic views of Vienna and the surrounding countryside.

The structure, built in 1775, was designed as a symbol of Habsburg military might and features classical columns and arches. Visitors can climb to the top of the Gloriette for breathtaking views of the city.

Gloriette | Gloriette

Address: Schönbrunner Schloßstraße 47, 1130 Vienna

Public transport: U4 to Schönbrunn

Opening hours: Daily: 9 a.m. – 6 p.m.

Online: www.schoenbrunn.at/en/

The Palm House: The Palm House is a magnificent Victorian-style glasshouse that houses exotic plants from around the world. Built in 1882, it is one of the largest greenhouses in Europe and is divided into three climate zones: tropical, subtropical, and temperate. The Palm House is a must-visit for plant lovers and offers a peaceful retreat within the palace gardens.

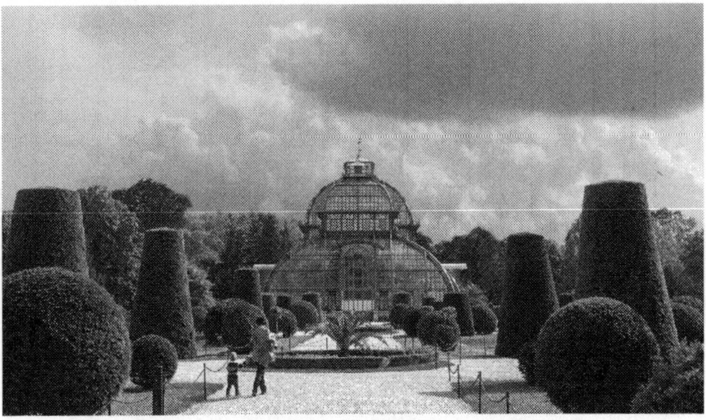

The Palm House

Palmenhaus | The Palm House

Address: Schönbrunner Schloßstraße 47, 1130 Vienna

Public transport: U4 to Schönbrunn

Opening hours: Daily: 9 a.m. – 5 p.m.

www.bundesgaerten.at/schlosspark-schoenbrunn/das-grosse-palmenhaus.html

Curiosity: The Schönbrunn Orangery, located on the eastern side of the gardens, was one of the largest orangeries in Europe when it was built in the 18th century. It was used to house citrus trees and other exotic plants during the winter months and was a symbol of the Habsburgs' wealth and refinement.

The Schönbrunn Zoo (Tiergarten Schönbrunn)

Estimated time: 1.5-2 hours

Schönbrunn Palace is home to the Schönbrunn Zoo, the oldest zoo in the world, founded in 1752 by Emperor Francis I, the husband of Maria Theresa. The zoo was originally designed as an imperial menagerie and has since grown into one of the most respected zoos in Europe, with a focus on conservation and education.

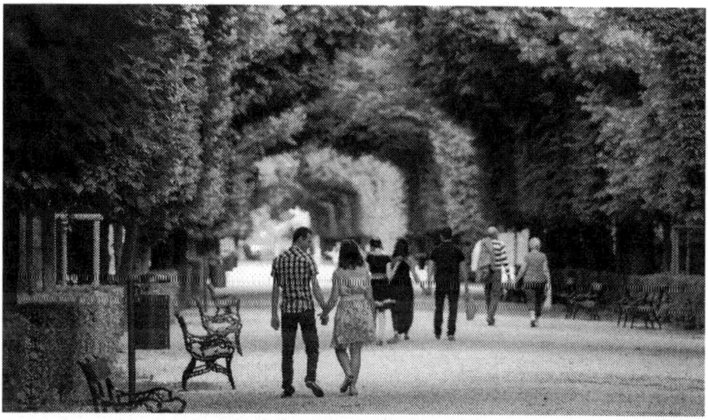

The Schönbrunn Gardens

Key highlights include:

The Giant Pandas: Schönbrunn Zoo is famous for its giant pandas, one of the few places outside China where these endangered animals can be seen. The pandas are part of an international breeding program aimed at protecting the species from extinction.

The Rainforest House: The Rainforest House is an immersive exhibit that recreates the environment of a tropical rainforest, complete with exotic plants, birds, reptiles, and mammals. Visitors can walk through the dense foliage and experience the sights and sounds of the jungle.

The Polarium: The Polarium is home to polar animals, including penguins and seals. The exhibit is designed to mimic the animals' natural habitats, offering visitors a close-up look at these fascinating creatures.

Curiosity: The Schönbrunn Zoo was originally designed as a private pleasure garden for the imperial family, but it was opened to the public in the 18th century. Today, it is recognized for its efforts in species conservation and was named the Best Zoo in Europe in 2018.

Tiergarten Schönbrunn | The Schönbrunn Zoo

Address: Maxingstraße 13b, 1130 Vienna

Public transport: U4 to Schönbrunn

Opening hours: Daily: 9 a.m. – 4:30 p.m.

Online: www.zoovienna.at/en/

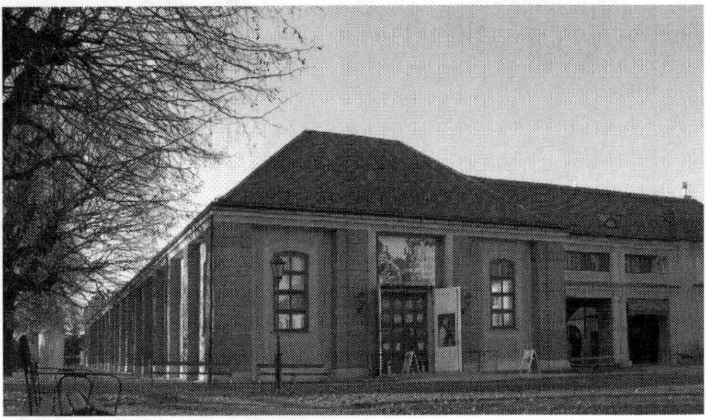

The Carriage Museum (Wagenburg)

The Carriage Museum (Wagenburg)

Estimated time: 45 minutes - 1 hour

Located near the palace, the Carriage Museum (Wagenburg) offers a fascinating glimpse into the world of imperial transportation. The museum's collection includes over 60 carriages, sleighs, and sedan chairs used by the Habsburgs for state occasions, weddings, and funerals.

Key highlights include:

The Coronation Coach: One of the most impressive items in the collection is the Imperial Coronation Coach, an ornate, gilded carriage that was used for the coronations of Habsburg emperors.

The coach is adorned with symbols of imperial power, including eagles, laurel wreaths, and allegorical figures.

Sisi's Carriages: The museum also features several carriages used by Empress Elisabeth (Sisi), including a lightweight travel coach that reflects her love of speed and adventure.

The museum's exhibits provide insight into Sisi's personality and her distaste for the formalities of imperial life.

Curiosity: The museum also displays the carriage that carried Napoleon's son, known as the Duke of Reichstadt, when he lived in Schönbrunn after Napoleon's defeat.

The carriage is a reminder of the palace's role in European political history.

Wagenburg | The Carriage Museum

Address: Schloss Schönbrunn, 1130 Vienna

Public transport: U4 to Schönbrunn

Opening hours: Daily: 9 a.m. – 5 p.m.

Online: www.kaiserliche-wagenburg.at/en/

Exploring the Surrounding Area

The area surrounding Schönbrunn Palace offers additional opportunities for exploration, from charming neighborhoods to cozy cafés with stunning views of the palace grounds.

Hietzinger Friedhof

Location: Adjacent to Schönbrunn Palace

Walking distance: 15 minutes

Hietzinger Friedhof | Hietzinger Cemetery

Address: Maxingstraße 15, 1130 Vienna

Public transport: U4 to Hietzing

Opening hours: Daily: 9 a.m. – 7 p.m.

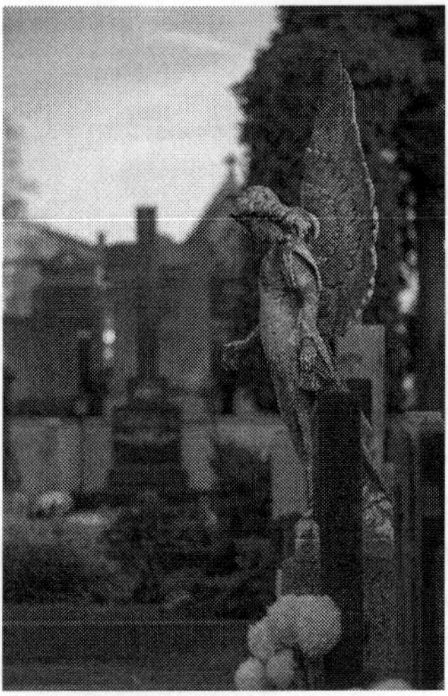

Hietzinger Friedhof

Hietzinger Friedhof is one of the city's most famous cemeteries. Known for its serene atmosphere and beautifully landscaped grounds, it is a place where many of Vienna's elite and historically significant figures are buried.

This cemetery reflects Vienna's rich cultural and intellectual history, as it is the final resting place for famous artists, musicians, scientists, and politicians who shaped the city's identity and legacy.

Hietzinger Friedhof was established in 1787, making it one of the older cemeteries in Vienna. It is located in the affluent Hietzing district, which is adjacent to Schönbrunn Palace and has historically been home to Vienna's aristocracy and upper classes.

Due to its location, many prominent individuals who lived in Hietzing or had connections to Vienna's elite were buried here.

The cemetery is known for its simple layout and its focus on providing a peaceful, green space for mourning and remembrance. The headstones and mausoleums vary in style, reflecting the personal tastes and historical periods in which they were erected.

From simple grave markers to grand, ornate tombs, the cemetery's design mirrors Vienna's evolution as a cultural and intellectual hub.

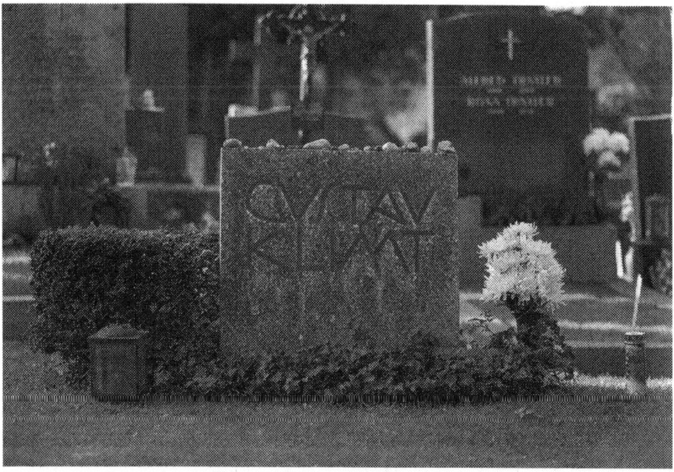

Gustav Klimt (1862-1918)

Gustav Klimt, one of the most important and influential artists in Austrian history, is buried in Hietzinger Friedhof. Klimt was a leading figure in the Vienna Secession, a movement that sought to break away from traditional academic art and embrace modern, innovative forms of expression. His paintings are known for their symbolic, often erotic imagery, and his use of gold leaf and intricate patterns.

Klimt's most famous works include "The Kiss", which is housed in the Belvedere Palace, and "Portrait of Adele Bloch-Bauer I", which became the subject of international interest during restitution claims following World War II. Klimt died in 1918 after suffering a stroke, and his grave in Hietzinger Friedhof is frequently visited by art lovers from around the world.

Otto Wagner, one of Vienna's most important architects, is also buried in Hietzinger Friedhof. Wagner was a pioneer of modern architecture and played a crucial role in the development of the city's urban landscape.

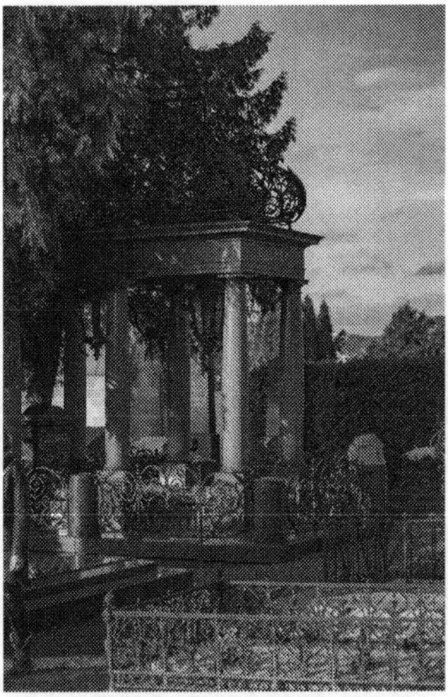
Otto Wagner (1841–1918)

His work marked a shift from the ornate historicism of the 19th century to the cleaner, more functional lines of modern design.

Wagner's most notable buildings include the Vienna Stadtbahn (city railway) stations, the Church of St. Leopold (Kirche am Steinhof), and the Postsparkasse (Postal Savings Bank). He was a professor at the Academy of Fine Arts in Vienna, where he influenced a generation of architects, including Josef Hoffmann. Wagner's tomb, like his architecture, reflects his modernist ideals, with a simple, elegant design that contrasts with some of the more elaborate graves in the cemetery.

Franz Grillparzer (1791–1872)

Franz Grillparzer is one of Austria's most celebrated playwrights and poets, known for his works that explore themes of fate, identity, and national history. His plays, such as "The Ahnfrau" and "King Ottokar's Fortune and End", are considered masterpieces of German-language drama.

Grillparzer's grave is a significant site in Hietzinger Friedhof, and his legacy as a national literary figure has made him a lasting symbol of Austrian cultural pride. Visitors to his grave often reflect on his contributions to Austrian identity during a time of significant political and social change in the 19th century.

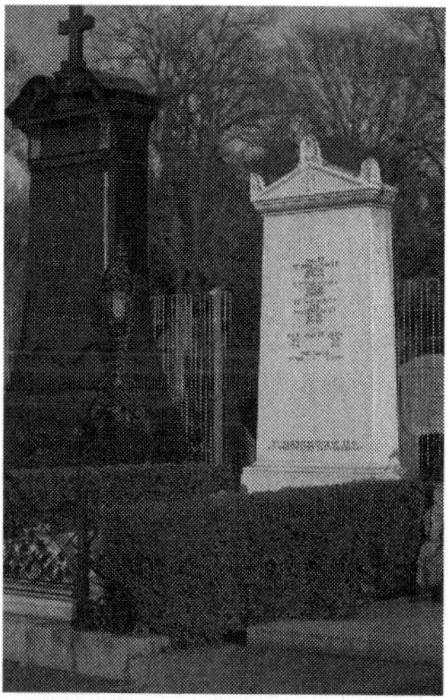

Koloman Moser (1868–1918)

Koloman Moser was a multifaceted artist and designer who was instrumental in the development of the Vienna Secession and the Wiener Werkstätte, movements that sought to bring modernism to the decorative arts, architecture, and design. Moser was born in Vienna in 1868 and studied at the Vienna Academy of Fine Arts and the School of Applied Arts. Along with Gustav Klimt, Josef Hoffmann, and others, he co-founded the Vienna Secession in 1897, a group that rebelled against the academic norms of art in favor of innovative, experimental designs that reflected the modern world.

Moser's work spanned a wide range of mediums, including painting, graphic design, furniture, and textiles. He was one of the key figures behind the founding of the Wiener Werkstätte in 1903, a production community of visual artists that aimed to unify art and craft in everyday objects, making beauty accessible in all aspects of life. His bold, geometric patterns and distinctive Art Nouveau style became iconic, influencing the development of modern design in Europe.

Notable works by Moser include:

His role in designing the Steinhof Church (Church of St. Leopold) alongside Otto Wagner, where Moser created the stained glass windows and interior designs.

His graphic designs for Ver Sacrum, the official magazine of the Vienna Secession.

Furniture, textiles, and jewelry for the Wiener Werkstätte that have since become symbols of early modernist design.

Koloman Moser's Grave: Moser's grave is located in Hietzinger Friedhof, near some of Vienna's most prominent cultural figures. The headstone is elegant yet modest, reflecting his contribution to modern design without the need for ornate decoration. Visitors to his grave come to honor a man whose designs helped shape the face of modern European art and whose influence can still be seen in contemporary design today.

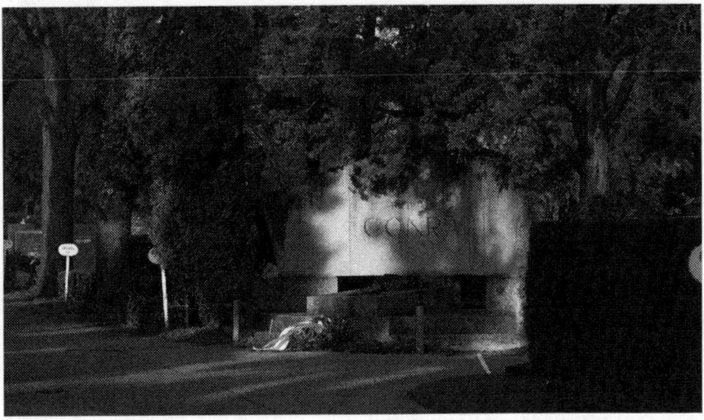

Franz Conrad von Hötzendorf (1852–1925)

Franz Conrad von Hötzendorf was a central figure in the Austro-Hungarian military during the early 20th century, particularly known for his role as Chief of the General Staff during World War I. Born in Penzing, now part of Vienna, Conrad came from a military family and entered the Theresian Military Academy at the age of 14. He rose through the ranks and became one of the most influential military leaders in the Austro-Hungarian Empire.

Conrad's career was marked by his aggressive strategic views and his push for a more offensive military stance. He was a staunch advocate of preemptive strikes, particularly against Serbia and Italy, which he viewed as threats to the stability of the Austro-Hungarian Empire. His role in shaping military policy leading up to and during World War I was significant, though his strategies have since been widely debated by historians, with some criticizing his over-reliance on offensive tactics in a war that demanded more flexible responses.

Despite his controversial military strategies, Conrad was respected as a patriotic and dedicated soldier, deeply committed to the survival of the Austro-Hungarian Empire. After the empire's dissolution following World War I, Conrad retired from military service and lived a quieter life until his death in 1925.

Franz Conrad von Hötzendorf's Grave: Conrad's grave can be found in Hietzinger Friedhof, where it is a monument to his military career and the role he played in one of the most turbulent periods of European history. His grave features a striking stone cross and is inscribed with his military rank and honors, reflecting the high regard in which he was held by his contemporaries. Visitors to Conrad's grave often reflect on the complexities of his legacy, as both a dedicated military leader and a figure whose strategies contributed to the immense human cost of World War I.

Katharina Schratt (1853–1940)

Katharina Schratt was one of the most famous actresses of her time and is remembered not only for her theatrical career but also for her close relationship with Emperor Franz Joseph I. Born in Baden bei Wien in 1853, Schratt became a prominent figure on the Viennese stage, gaining fame for her roles in classical and contemporary plays. She was admired for her beauty, charm, and stage presence, which made her a favorite among Viennese theatergoers and members of high society.

However, Schratt is most famous for her close personal relationship with Emperor Franz Joseph, which began in the 1880s. Although their relationship was never officially acknowledged as romantic, it was widely known that Schratt was a close confidante and companion to the emperor, particularly after the death of his wife, Empress Elisabeth (Sisi), in 1898. Franz Joseph would visit Schratt almost daily, and their friendship provided him with much-needed emotional support in the final years of his reign.

Schratt lived a relatively quiet life after the death of the emperor in 1916, withdrawing from public view. She died in 1940 and was buried in Hietzinger Friedhof, where her grave is a site of interest for those fascinated by the personal lives of the Habsburgs and their inner circle.

Katharina Schratt's Grave: Schratt's grave is modest, reflecting her personal character and the discretion with which she managed her relationship with the emperor. The headstone includes her name, dates of birth and death, and a simple cross. Her grave is often visited by those intrigued by the relationship between Franz Joseph and Schratt, which has become part of the folklore surrounding the Habsburg monarchy.

Lainzer Friedhof

Lainzer Friedhof, located in the tranquil district of Hietzing, close to the more famous Hietzinger Friedhof, is a relatively small but historically significant cemetery in Vienna. It is best known as the final resting place of Sir Karl Popper, one of the most influential philosophers of the 20th century. The cemetery offers a peaceful environment for reflection and is a place where visitors can pay homage to one of the greatest minds in modern philosophy, as well as other notable individuals from Vienna's history.

Sir Karl Popper (1902–1994) was born in Vienna in 1902 and became one of the most important and influential philosophers of the 20th century. Known for his contributions to the philosophy of science, particularly his theory of falsifiability, Popper's work had a profound impact on scientific thought and methodology. He argued that scientific theories can never be proven definitively but must be subject to continuous testing and should be regarded as valid only until they are falsified.

Popper was also a political philosopher who strongly advocated for open societies and the protection of individual freedoms. His opposition to totalitarianism, fascism, and communism is articulated in his seminal political work "The Open Society and Its Enemies", which critiqued historicism and the belief in inevitable historical progress. Popper's intellectual legacy extends beyond philosophy into fields such as political science, economics, and the social sciences.

Popper spent much of his academic career in the United Kingdom, particularly at the London School of Economics, where he taught and developed his most influential ideas. He was knighted in 1965 for his services to philosophy and was awarded numerous honors and recognitions throughout his life. Despite his global influence, Popper retained strong ties to Austria and Vienna, where he returned later in life. Upon his death in 1994, Popper was buried in Lainzer Friedhof, in the city where he was born and where his intellectual journey began.

Lainzer Friedhof | Lainzer Cemetery

Address: Friedenszeile 2, 1130 Vienna

Public transport: U4 to Hietzing, then bus 56A

Opening hours: Daily: 7a.m. – 7 p.m.

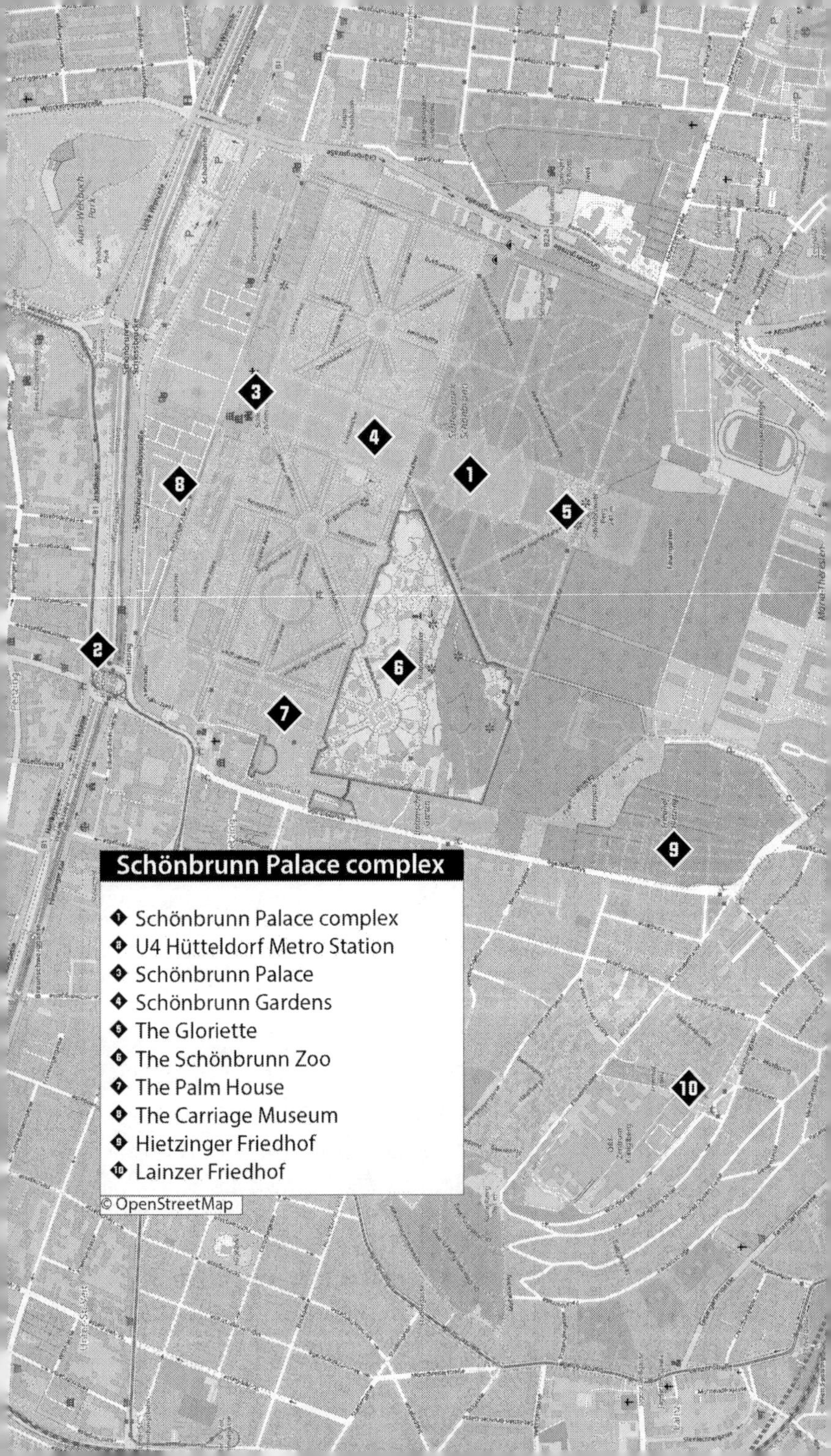
Schönbrunn Palace complex
1 Schönbrunn Palace complex
2 U4 Hütteldorf Metro Station
3 Schönbrunn Palace
4 Schönbrunn Gardens
5 The Gloriette
6 The Schönbrunn Zoo
7 The Palm House
8 The Carriage Museum
9 Hietzinger Friedhof
10 Lainzer Friedhof
© OpenStreetMap

THE VIENNA SECESSION

The Vienna Secession, founded in 1897, was a revolutionary artistic movement that profoundly reshaped the cultural landscape of Vienna at the turn of the 20th century. Breaking away from the traditional academic art institutions of the time, the Secessionists sought to redefine art, rejecting historical styles and embracing new, innovative forms of expression. At the heart of this movement was a desire to create a bridge between fine arts and applied arts, to blur the boundaries between art and life, and to capture the spirit of modernity in a rapidly changing world.

Under the leadership of Gustav Klimt, the Vienna Secession became a hub for some of the most progressive artists, architects, and designers of the era. Their influence spread beyond Austria, contributing to the broader European movements of Art Nouveau and Symbolism. The legacy of the Secession can still be felt in Vienna today, particularly in the iconic Secession Building and the radical works that continue to inspire contemporary artists.

Origins of the Vienna Secession: Breaking with Tradition

In the late 19th century, Vienna's art scene was dominated by the Künstlerhaus, the official association of Austrian artists. The Künstlerhaus was a conservative institution, adhering to traditional academic standards of art, which focused heavily on historical themes, classical techniques, and representational accuracy.

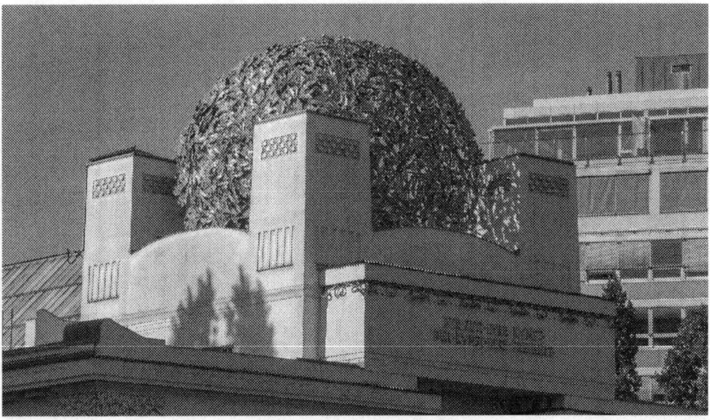

The Secession Building

Many young and progressive artists felt that the rigid framework imposed by the Künstlerhaus stifled creativity and prevented them from exploring new artistic ideas that were emerging across Europe.

By the 1890s, the winds of change were sweeping through European art, influenced by movements such as Impressionism, Symbolism, and the Arts and Crafts movement. These new directions challenged the traditional boundaries of art, emphasizing emotion, symbolism, and abstraction over mere technical mastery. In Vienna, a group of forward-thinking artists grew increasingly frustrated with the constraints of the academic art establishment and sought to establish a platform where innovative and experimental art could thrive.

In 1897, led by Gustav Klimt, a group of 19 artists—including notable figures such as Koloman Moser, Josef Hoffmann, and Carl Moll—broke away from the Künstlerhaus to form the Vienna Secession. The group's primary goal was to create an open and independent forum for modern art, free from the strictures of academic tradition.

They aimed to promote the avant-garde and to showcase works that reflected the new artistic ideals of the fin-de-siècle period.

The Secessionists were not bound by a single style or aesthetic. Instead, they embraced a wide range of artistic expressions, from painting and sculpture to architecture and decorative arts. Their motto, "To every age its art, to art its freedom," encapsulated their belief that each era should have the liberty to define its own artistic identity.

The Secession Building: A Temple of Modern Art

One of the most enduring symbols of the Vienna Secession is the Secession Building (Secessionsgebäude), which was completed in 1898. Designed by the architect Joseph Maria Olbrich, the building itself was a radical departure from the traditional neoclassical architecture that dominated Vienna at the time. With its clean lines, white walls, and the now iconic golden dome of laurel leaves, the Secession Building embodied the ideals of the movement: simplicity, modernity, and the fusion of art and design.

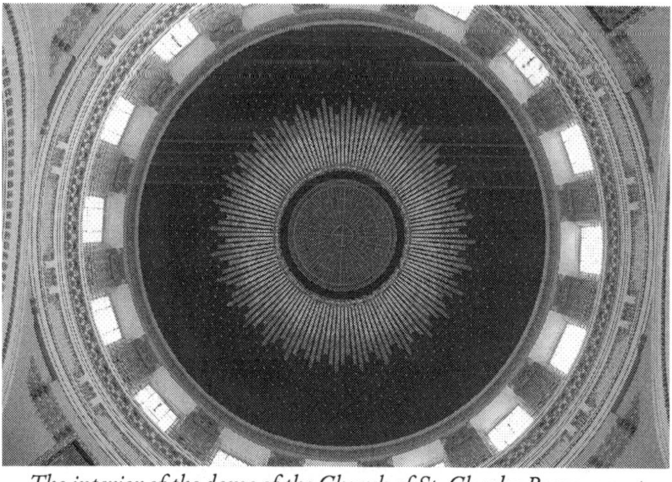

The interior of the dome of the Church of St. Charles Borromeo at Vienna's Zentralfriedhof was designed by architect Max Hegele (1911).

The building was conceived as more than just a gallery; it was a manifesto in architectural form. It provided a space where modern artists could exhibit their works without the constraints of conservative institutions. The Secession Building became a center for artistic innovation, hosting exhibitions that showcased the latest trends in art from Vienna and abroad. The building's facade bears the inscription "Der Zeit ihre Kunst, der Kunst ihre Freiheit" ("To every age its art, to art its freedom"), a declaration of the Secessionists' commitment to artistic autonomy.

Inside the Secession Building, one of the most famous works of the movement is displayed: Gustav Klimt's Beethoven Frieze. This monumental work, created for the 14th Secession exhibition in 1902, is a tribute to Ludwig van Beethoven and his Ninth Symphony. The frieze, which spans three walls, is a highly symbolic and expressive work that explores themes of human suffering, desire, and redemption. Klimt's use of allegorical figures, intricate patterns, and shimmering gold leaf makes the Beethoven Frieze one of the most significant examples of Symbolist art in the Secessionist style.

The Artists of the Vienna Secession

While Klimt is perhaps the most famous artist associated with the Vienna Secession, the movement was a collective effort that included a wide range of artists, designers, and architects, each contributing to its revolutionary spirit.

Gustav Klimt played a central role in the Secession, not only as a leader but also as a visionary artist whose work encapsulated the movement's ideals. Klimt's early works, such as the murals in the Burgtheater and the Kunsthistorisches Museum, reflected a more academic style, but his later work broke away from convention. His sensual and often provocative depictions of the human form, particularly his portrayals of women, were groundbreaking for their psychological depth and use of symbolism. Klimt's Golden Period, during which he created masterpieces like "The Kiss" and "Portrait of Adele Bloch-Bauer I", is closely associated with the aesthetic ideals of the Secession.

Koloman Moser was another key figure in the movement, known for his versatility across different artistic media. Moser was not only a painter but also a designer who contributed to the applied arts, creating textiles, furniture, and graphic designs that reflected the Secessionist emphasis on the unity of art and design. He was a founding member of the Wiener Werkstätte, an offshoot of the Secession that focused on high-quality craftsmanship and design in everyday objects, promoting the idea that art should be integrated into all aspects of life.

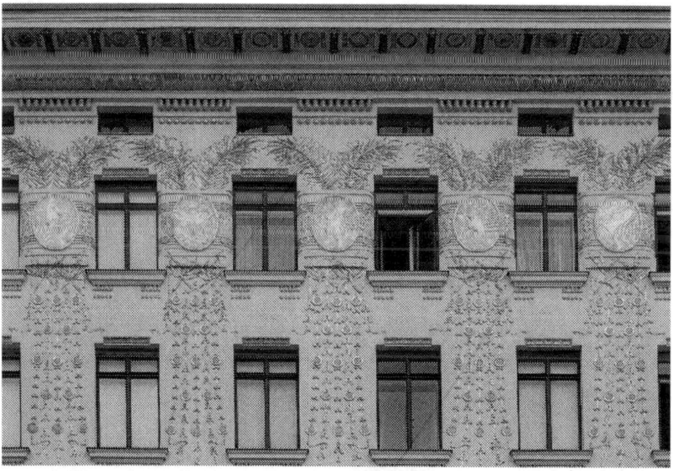

Medallions by Koloman Moser on the Facade of Linke Wienzeile 38, Vienna

Josef Hoffmann, an architect and designer, also played a pivotal role in the Vienna Secession. His work exemplified the movement's ideals of modernity and simplicity. Hoffmann's designs, such as the Palais Stoclet in Brussels, merged art with architecture, creating holistic environments where every detail, from the structure to the furnishings, was carefully considered. Hoffmann was also a co-founder of the Wiener Werkstätte, further advancing the Secession's mission to blur the lines between fine art and applied art.

Otto Wagner was a visionary architect and a central figure in Vienna's transition to modernism. Known for his forward-thinking approach, Wagner embraced new materials like steel and glass, and championed functional design over decorative excess. His work spanned from urban infrastructure projects, such as the Stadtbahn, to architectural masterpieces like the Postal Savings Bank. Wagner was a key advocate for modern architecture, rejecting historical styles in favor of simplicity and utility. His influence extended beyond individual buildings, shaping the future of architecture in Vienna and setting the stage for modernist movements like Bauhaus.

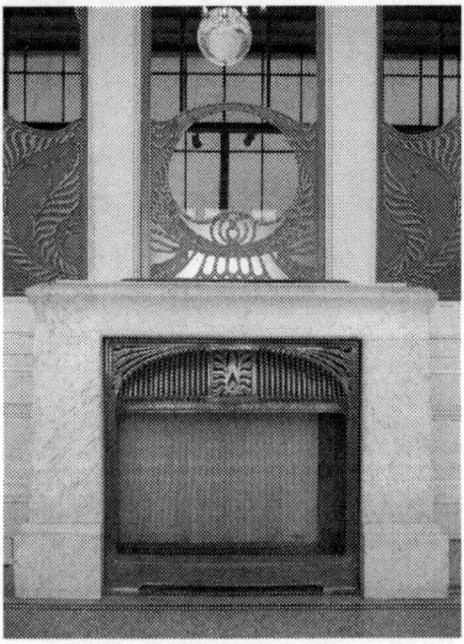

Interior of the Kaiserpavillon by Otto Wagner (1899)

The Secession was not limited to visual artists. Writers, composers, and intellectuals, including figures such as Sigmund Freud and Arnold Schoenberg, were also connected to the broader cultural movement that the Secession represented. The turn of the century in Vienna was a time of radical intellectual and artistic ferment, and the Secession provided a forum where new ideas could be explored and shared.

The Secession and Art Nouveau

The Vienna Secession was part of a broader European movement that sought to break with historical traditions and embrace modernity. The Secessionists were closely aligned with the international Art

Nouveau movement, which emphasized organic forms, flowing lines, and the integration of art into everyday life. In many ways, the Vienna Secession was the Austrian counterpart to the Jugendstil movement in Germany and the Art Nouveau movement in France and Belgium.

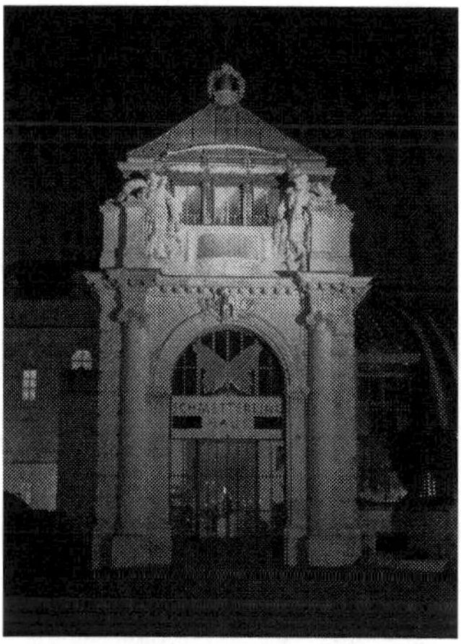

The Butterfly House (Schmetterling Haus) in the Burggarten is part of the Palm House, designed by Friedrich Ohmann (1902–1906).

However, while Art Nouveau was often associated with decorative excess and the use of elaborate ornamentation, the Vienna Secessionists tended to favor more restrained and geometric designs. This is particularly evident in the work of architects like Josef Hoffmann and Otto Wagner, whose buildings emphasized clean lines and functional beauty.

The Secessionists also differed from their Art Nouveau counterparts in their emphasis on symbolism and psychological depth. While many Art Nouveau works focused on natural beauty and aesthetic pleasure, the Vienna Secessionists were more interested in exploring complex human emotions and the darker aspects of the human experience. This is particularly true of Klimt's later work, which delved into themes of sexuality, death, and the subconscious.

Museum für Angewandte Kunst | Museum of Applied Arts

Historical Significance: The museum houses an extensive collection of Wiener Werkstätte works, showcasing the craftsmanship and design innovations that defined early 20th-century Viennese art. These exhibits highlight the movement's philosophy of integrating art into everyday life, with pieces ranging from textiles and furniture to ceramics and graphic design.

Address: Stubenring 5, 1010 Vienna

Public transport: U3 to Stubentor

Hours: Tue-Sun 10 a.m. – 6 p.m.

Online: www.mak.at

Otto Wagner Museum

Historical Significance: Located in the historic Karlsplatz station, this museum is dedicated to the works and legacy of Otto Wagner. It offers an in-depth look at his revolutionary designs, from urban projects like the Stadtbahn to his groundbreaking architectural works, highlighting his pivotal role in the transformation of Vienna into a modern city.

Address: Karlsplatz, 1040 Vienna

Public transport: U1, U2, U4 to Karlsplatz

Hours: Check the website for opening hours

www.wienmuseum.at/otto_wagner_pavillon_karlsplatz_en

Belvedere | Austrian Gallery Belvedere

Historical Significance: The Belvedere houses one of the largest collections of Gustav Klimt's works, including his world-famous painting "The Kiss." This iconic masterpiece, along with other works from his Golden Period, represents Klimt's exploration of sensuality, beauty, and modern artistic expression, solidifying his place in art history.

Address: Prinz Eugen-Straße 27, 1030 Vienna

Public transport: Tram D to Schloss Belvedere

Hours: Daily 10 a.m. – 6 p.m.

Online: www.belvedere.at

GUSTAV KLIMT

Gustav Klimt, one of the most prominent figures in Vienna's cultural history, remains a defining artist whose influence on modern art still resonates. Born in 1862 in Baumgarten, a suburb of Vienna, Klimt grew up during a time of significant artistic and intellectual flourishing in the Austrian capital. His work, steeped in symbolism, eroticism, and innovation, has become synonymous with Vienna's fin-de-siècle period. Klimt's legacy can still be felt throughout the city, from his most iconic masterpieces in museums to his role in the Viennese Secessionist movement, which helped redefine the boundaries of modern art.

Early Life and Education

Klimt was born into a family with modest means. His father, a gold engraver, and his mother, a talented but frustrated musician, both influenced his early artistic sensibilities. Recognizing Gustav's talent at a young age, his family encouraged him to apply to the Vienna School of Arts and Crafts (Kunstgewerbeschule), which he entered at just 14. Here, Klimt trained in the classical tradition, learning skills that would lay the foundation for his future career as a painter and muralist.

Early in his career, Klimt, along with his brother Ernst and fellow artist Franz Matsch, founded the Künstler-Compagnie (Artists' Company). Together, they worked on commissions to decorate public buildings, including theaters and museums. Their classical style was well-received, particularly the murals they created for the Burgtheater and the Kunsthistorisches Museum in Vienna.

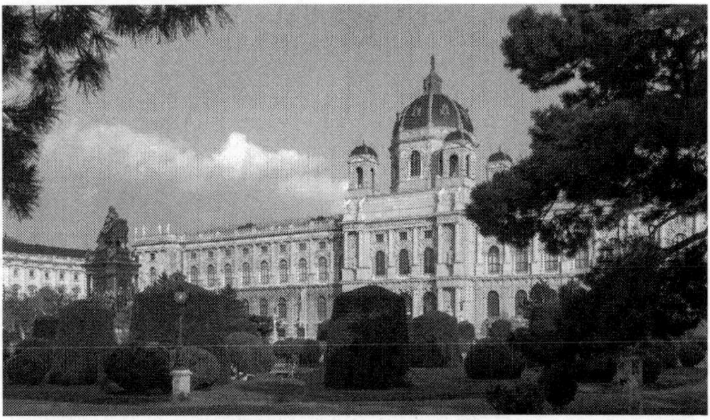

Kunsthistorisches Museum (KHM)

The Viennese Secession: Breaking Away

In 1897, dissatisfied with the conservative art establishment in Vienna, Klimt became one of the founding members of the Vienna Secession. This avant-garde movement sought to challenge the academic traditions that dominated the art world at the time. The Secessionists believed that art should not be confined to historical themes or rigid aesthetic rules but should embrace new forms of expression and tap into deeper psychological and emotional realms.

Klimt became the first president of the Vienna Secession and served as its leader during its early years. The group's motto, "To every age its art, to art its freedom," perfectly encapsulated Klimt's evolving philosophy. Under his guidance, the Secessionists broke away from traditional art forms and explored more symbolic and expressive methods, combining elements of Symbolism, Art Nouveau, and even Japonism into their work. The movement's central exhibition space, the Secession Building (Secessionsgebäude), remains one of Vienna's most iconic architectural landmarks, with Klimt's famous Beethoven Frieze housed within.

Klimt's Golden Period and Iconic Works

Klimt's artistic breakthrough came during what is known as his "Golden Period," where he incorporated gold leaf into his paintings. His fascination with Byzantine mosaics influenced this unique technique, particularly those he saw during a trip to Ravenna, Italy. His use of gold leaf and intricate patterns gave his works a shimmering, ethereal quality that captivated viewers.

Perhaps the most famous painting from this period is "The Kiss" (1907-1908), which today is one of the most celebrated and recognizable works of art in the world. This painting, housed in Vienna's Belvedere Palace, depicts a couple locked in an intimate embrace, enveloped in gold and intricate patterns that blur the lines between the figures and their surroundings. "The Kiss" has come to symbolize love, sensuality, and beauty, making it one of Klimt's most enduring masterpieces.

Other important works from Klimt's Golden Period include "Portrait of Adele Bloch-Bauer I" (1907), a stunning portrayal of a Viennese socialite that also prominently features gold leaf. This painting became famously known as "The Lady in Gold" after being at the center of a lengthy legal battle over Nazi-looted art. Today, it hangs in New York's Neue Galerie, but its creation and significance remain deeply tied to Klimt's life in Vienna.

Eroticism and Feminine Power

Klimt's work was often controversial in its time, particularly due to his overt depiction of the female form and sensuality. Many of his portraits and allegorical works feature women in poses that were considered scandalous for the time. Klimt explored themes of eroticism and the psychological complexity of his female subjects, which led to frequent criticism from conservative Viennese society. His series of paintings known as the "Faculty Paintings", intended for the ceiling of the University of Vienna, were particularly controversial due to their overt sexuality and symbolism. The university rejected them, and they were never installed.

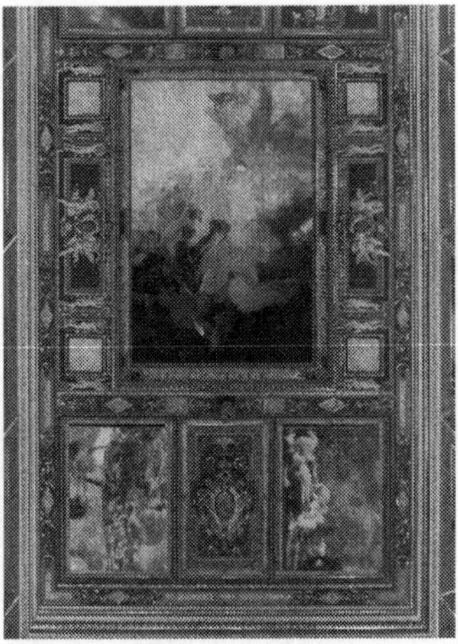

The reproductions of Gustav Klimt's ceiling paintings, The Main Ceremonial Hall, University of Vienna.

Women were central to Klimt's artistic vision, not just as muses but as powerful, autonomous figures. His depictions of women ranged from regal portraits of society's elite to mythological figures charged with erotic energy. Klimt's female subjects are often portrayed as sensual, enigmatic, and empowered, challenging the traditional representations of women in art during that era.

Despite the controversy, Klimt continued to be a favorite among Vienna's upper class, particularly with wealthy women who commissioned portraits from him. His work bridged the gap between fine art and decorative art, combining symbolic imagery with ornamental patterns and luxurious materials.

Klimt's Later Years and Death

In the later years of his life, Klimt's style evolved once more, moving away from the heavy use of gold leaf and towards a lighter, more fluid aesthetic. His landscapes, which are less well-known than his portraits and allegorical works, offer a glimpse into his changing artistic perspective. These paintings, often depicting peaceful scenes of the Austrian countryside, are marked by their vivid use of color and intricate patterns.

Gustav Klimt passed away unexpectedly in 1918 following a stroke at the age of 55. His death marked the end of an era, as he was one of many prominent figures lost during the final year of World War I. Klimt's influence endured through contemporaries and successors like Egon Schiele and Oskar Kokoschka.

Burgtheater | Vienna's National Theater

Historical Significance: Klimt, his brother Ernst, and Franz Matsch painted ceiling murals here in the late 1880s, marking Klimt's early success. The staircase frescoes showcase his classical style before transitioning to Symbolism.

Address: Universitätsring 2, 1010 Vienna

Public transport: U2 to Schottentor

Hours: Guided tours available; check website for times

Online: www.burgtheater.at

Kunsthistorisches Museum | Museum of Art History

Historical Significance: The grand staircase ceiling paintings at the Kunsthistorisches Museum are an early work by Klimt, created with his brother and Franz Matsch. These mythological and allegorical scenes continue to captivate visitors.

Address: Maria-Theresien-Platz, 1010 Vienna

Public transport: U2, U3 to Volkstheater

Hours: Thu-Tue 10 a.m. – 6 p.m.

Online: www.khm.at

Secession | Vienna Secession Building

Historical Significance: Founded by Klimt and others in 1897, the Vienna Secession revolutionized art by rejecting tradition. Klimt's famed Beethoven Frieze, in the Secession's basement, embodies the movement's ideals.

Address: Friedrichstraße 12, 1010 Vienna

Public transport: U1, U2, U4 to Karlsplatz

Hours: Tue-Sun 10 a.m. – 6 p.m.

Online: www.secession.at

Belvedere | Upper Belvedere Palace

Historical Significance: The Belvedere houses one of the largest Klimt collections, including his iconic masterpiece *The Kiss* and other Golden Period works, showcased in the Upper Belvedere's Austrian art collection.

Address: Prinz Eugen-Straße 27, 1030 Vienna

Public transport: Tram D to Schloss Belvedere

Hours: Daily 10 a.m. – 6 p.m.

Online: www.belvedere.at

Theatermuseum | Theater Museum

Historical Significance: The Theatermuseum showcases Klimt's *Nuda Veritas* (1899), a bold painting symbolizing his break from tradition and his exploration of truth, beauty, and the human form.

Address: Lobkowitzplatz 2, 1010 Vienna

Public transport: U1, U3 to Stephansplatz

Hours: Daily 10 a.m. – 6 p.m.

Online: www.theatermuseum.at

Leopold Museum

Historical Significance: The Leopold Museum, known for Egon Schiele, also features Klimt's portraits, landscapes, and allegorical works, showcasing his influence and versatility. A must-visit for Klimt admirers.

Address: Museumsplatz 1, 1070 Vienna

Public transport: U2, U3 to Volkstheater

Hours: Daily 10 a.m. – 6 p.m.

Online: www.leopoldmuseum.org

Klimt Villa Wien | Klimt Villa

Historical Significance: This villa, Klimt's final studio from 1911 to 1918, saw the creation of many late masterpieces, including portraits and landscapes. Restored to reflect his workspace, it offers a unique glimpse into his creative process.

Address: Feldmühlgasse 11, 1130 Vienna

Public transport: U4 to Ober St. Veit, then Bus 54A or 54B to Klimt Villa

Hours: Wed-Sun 10 a.m. – 6 p.m.

Online: www.klimtvilla.at

Grave of Gustav Klim

Historical Significance: Gustav Klimt, a central figure of the Vienna Secession, is buried in Hietzing Cemetery. His grave can be found in Group 5, Grave 194.

Address: Maxingstraße 15, 1130 Vienna

Public transport: U4 to Hietzing

Hours: Daily, check website for seasonal times

Online: www.friedhoefewien.at

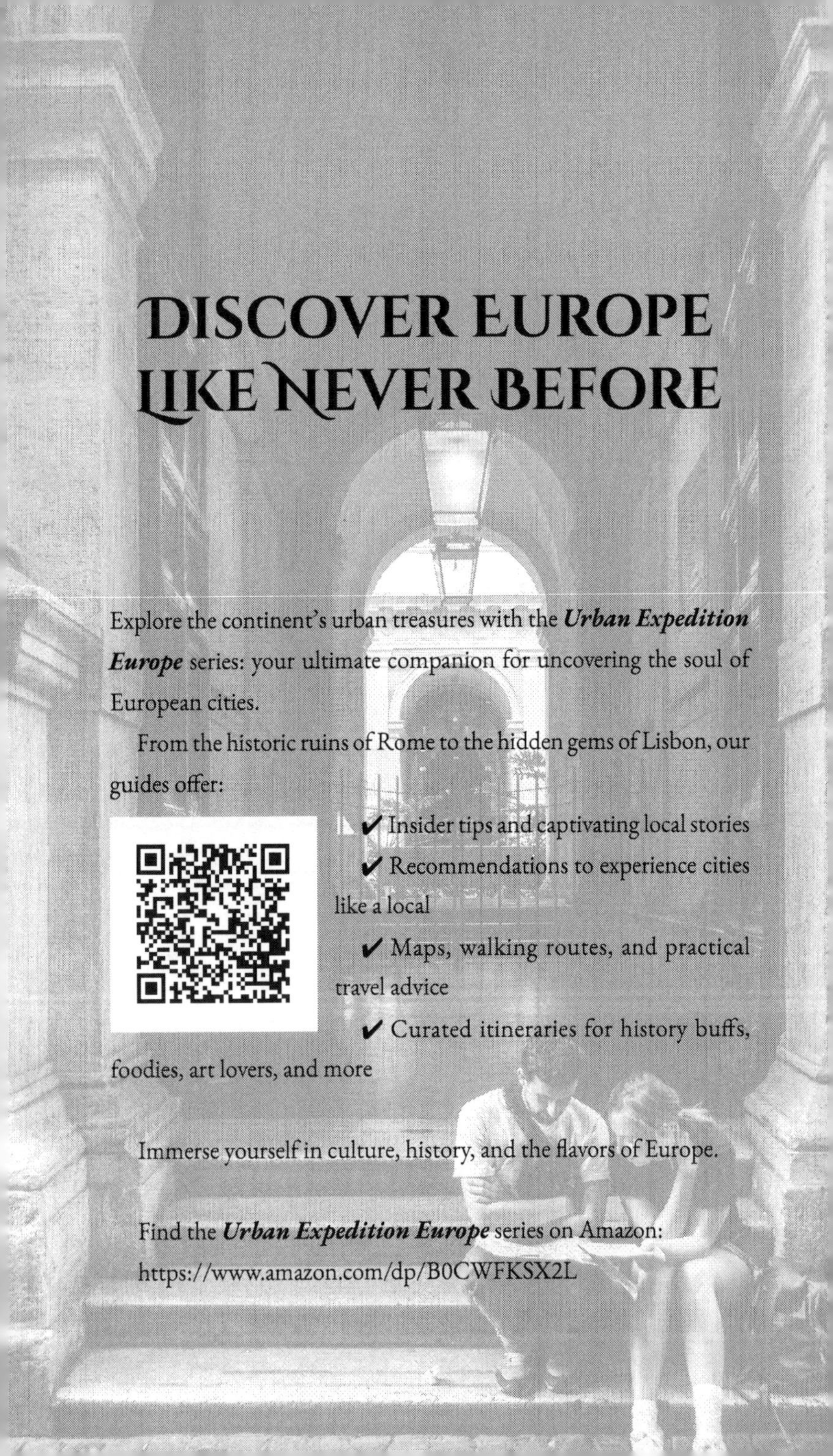
DISCOVER EUROPE LIKE NEVER BEFORE
Explore the continent's urban treasures with the ***Urban Expedition Europe*** series: your ultimate companion for uncovering the soul of European cities.
From the historic ruins of Rome to the hidden gems of Lisbon, our guides offer:
✔ Insider tips and captivating local stories
✔ Recommendations to experience cities like a local
✔ Maps, walking routes, and practical travel advice
✔ Curated itineraries for history buffs, foodies, art lovers, and more
Immerse yourself in culture, history, and the flavors of Europe.
Find the ***Urban Expedition Europe*** series on Amazon:
https://www.amazon.com/dp/B0CWFKSX2L

OTTO WAGNER

Otto Wagner (1841–1918) is one of Vienna's most celebrated architects, known for his visionary designs that bridged the 19th and 20th centuries and laid the groundwork for Modernism. Wagner was a key figure in Vienna's architectural evolution during a period of rapid industrialization and urban growth, and his influence on the city can still be seen in its striking buildings, innovative public infrastructure, and modern aesthetic principles. His designs were revolutionary for their functional simplicity, emphasis on practicality, and incorporation of modern materials like glass, steel, and concrete, rejecting the decorative excesses of the past.

As a professor, city planner, and practicing architect, Wagner not only left an indelible mark on the physical landscape of Vienna but also on its architectural philosophy, influencing generations of architects who followed him.

Early Career and Architectural Transition

Otto Wagner was born into a middle-class family in Vienna and showed an early talent for architecture. He studied at the Academy of Fine Arts in Vienna and later in Berlin, where he received a classical education in architecture. Wagner's early career was marked by traditional designs that adhered to the historicist styles popular in the mid-19th century. He worked on grand residential and commercial buildings in the eclectic style, drawing from classical, Gothic, Renaissance, and Baroque influences.

However, as Vienna transformed into a modern metropolis during the late 19th century, Wagner began to rethink his architectural philosophy. He grew increasingly critical of the ornamental and historicist styles that dominated the city's architecture and began to advocate for a more functional, modern approach that would reflect the needs of contemporary life. Wagner believed that architecture should be an expression of its time and that the old styles no longer served a purpose in a rapidly changing, industrialized society.

This shift in Wagner's thinking became more evident in the 1890s when he published "Moderne Architektur" (Modern Architecture), a manifesto that outlined his principles for modern design. In this influential work, Wagner rejected the imitation of historical styles and called for architecture that embraced functionality, modern materials, and simplicity of form. His famous quote, "What is impractical cannot be beautiful," encapsulated his belief that beauty in architecture should stem from utility and rationality, not merely decorative flourishes.

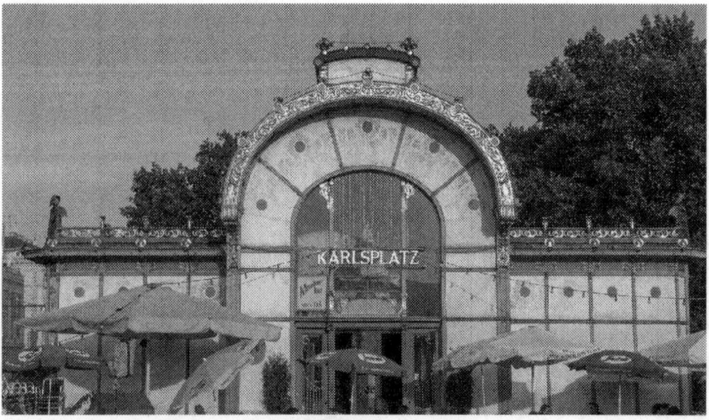

The Karlsplatz Pavilion

Wagner and the Urban Transformation of Vienna

During the late 19th century, Vienna underwent a significant transformation as part of the expansion project known as the Ringstraße. The old city walls were demolished, and in their place, a grand boulevard encircled the inner city, lined with monumental public buildings, palaces, and parks.

Wagner, who became involved in this city-wide redevelopment, saw this as an opportunity to bring his modern architectural vision to life.

One of Wagner's key contributions to Vienna's infrastructure was his role in designing the city's Stadtbahn (urban railway) system. His work on the Stadtbahn was not only a feat of engineering but also a showcase for his architectural philosophy. Wagner designed the railway stations along the line, incorporating modern materials like steel and glass, which allowed for light, air, and openness. The stations were functional yet elegant, featuring simple, geometric forms and minimal ornamentation, a radical departure from the heavily decorated historicist architecture that dominated Vienna at the time.

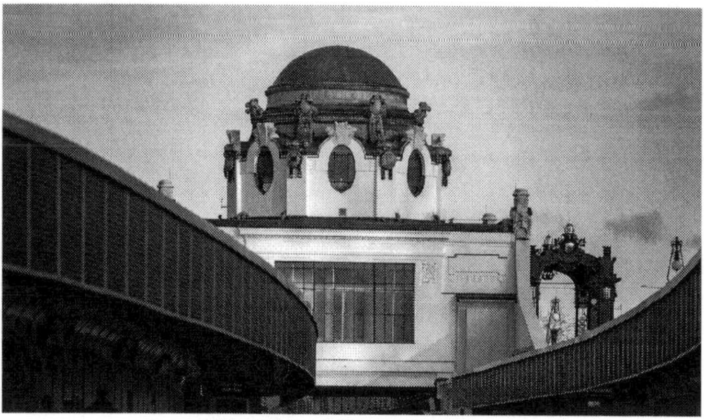

The Hofpavillon at Hietzing

Two of the most iconic stations from Wagner's Stadtbahn project are the Karlsplatz Pavilion and the Hofpavillon at Hietzing. The

Karlsplatz Pavilion, built in 1899, is a masterpiece of Viennese Art Nouveau (Jugendstil), with its green-and-white marble facade, decorative gold elements, and symmetrical design. While ornate compared to his later work, it represents Wagner's transition from historicism to modernism, blending aesthetic beauty with functional design. The Hofpavillon at Hietzing, a private station built for Emperor Franz Joseph, showcased Wagner's ability to combine modern materials with a sense of imperial grandeur.

The Secession and Modernist Architecture

Wagner was closely connected to the Vienna Secession, an artistic movement founded in 1897 by artists like Gustav Klimt and Koloman Moser, who sought to break away from the conservative traditions of the art world.

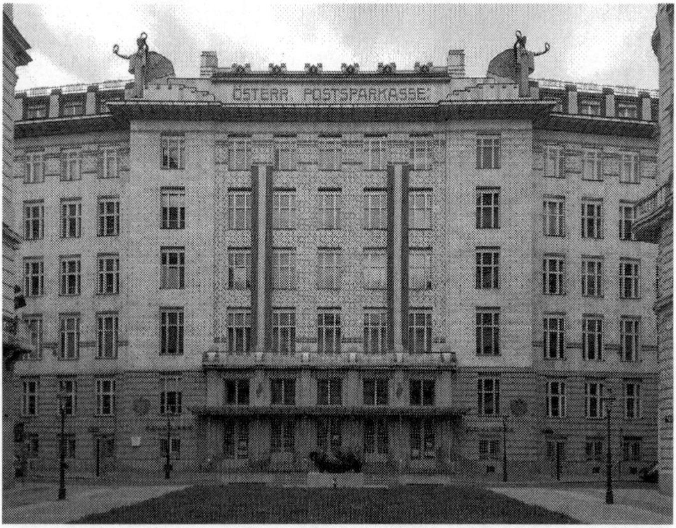

Postal Savings Bank

Wagner's later works were deeply influenced by the Secession's emphasis on simplicity, geometry, and clean lines. He began to experiment more boldly with new materials and construction techniques, using steel, concrete, and glass in ways that were unprecedented in Viennese architecture at the time. This modern approach is most evident in his design for the Postal Savings Bank (Postsparkasse), completed between 1903 and 1912, which remains one of his most iconic buildings.

The Postal Savings Bank is considered a landmark of early modern architecture. Located on the Ringstraße, the building exemplifies Wagner's philosophy of functional beauty. The exterior is clad in marble, but instead of using it for purely decorative purposes, Wagner attached the marble panels with visible aluminum rivets, emphasizing the building's structural logic and materials. Inside, the central banking hall is filled with natural light, thanks to a glass ceiling supported by steel beams.

The use of modern materials, minimal ornamentation, and emphasis on function made the Postal Savings Bank a groundbreaking building in the transition from historicism to modernism.

The Church at Steinhof: Sacred Modernism

One of Wagner's most remarkable works is the Church of St. Leopold at the Steinhof Psychiatric Hospital (also known as the Kirche am Steinhof). Completed in 1907, this church is often regarded as one of the first examples of modernist sacred architecture. Built on the outskirts of Vienna, the Church at Steinhof was commissioned as part of a larger hospital complex designed by Wagner, and it represents a bold departure from traditional church design.

The Church at Steinhof combines Wagner's commitment to modern materials and functional design with the spiritual and aesthetic demands of a sacred space. The building's dome, covered in gold leaf, shines against the Vienna skyline, while the white facade is simple and elegant, adorned with minimal decoration. Inside, Wagner used modern construction techniques to create an open, light-filled space that was practical for the needs of the hospital's patients, with ramps for easy access and ventilation for fresh air.

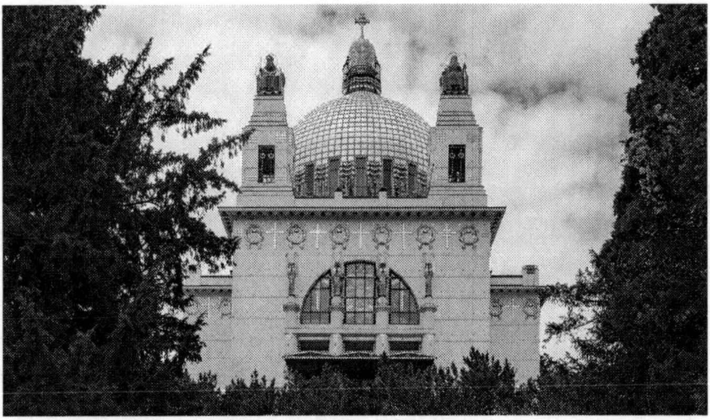

The Church at Steinhof

The church's interior is a stunning example of the synthesis of art and architecture. Wagner collaborated with artists like Koloman Moser to create a space that was both beautiful and serene. The stained-glass windows, mosaics, and altar all reflect the Viennese Secession's emphasis on geometric forms and the use of new materials, while the overall design emphasizes the functionality and simplicity that defined Wagner's later work.

Otto Wagner's Legacy in Vienna

Otto Wagner's impact on Vienna's architecture is profound and far-reaching. His embrace of modern materials, functional design, and simplicity helped to revolutionize architectural thinking in Vienna and beyond. Wagner's work laid the foundation for future architectural movements, particularly Modernism and Bauhaus, both of which championed many of the principles he introduced.

Pavilions at Karlsplatz | Otto Wagner's Stadtbahn Stations

Historical Significance: Otto Wagner designed these iconic Art Nouveau pavilions at Karlsplatz, prime examples of his early work on

Vienna's Stadtbahn. The pavilions showcase Wagner's use of modern materials like steel and glass, blending functionality with aesthetic elegance. They mark the beginning of Wagner's transition toward modernist design principles.

Address: Karlsplatz, 1040 Vienna

Public transport: U1, U2, U4 to Karlsplatz

Hours: Check the website for opening hours

Online: www.wienmuseum.at

Otto Wagner Church am Steinhof | Church of St. Leopold

Historical Significance: Built as part of the Steinhof Psychiatric Hospital complex, this groundbreaking church is one of Wagner's most significant works, blending sacred architecture with modernism. The Church of St. Leopold, with its gold dome and minimalist interior, is a masterpiece of form and function, offering a glimpse into Wagner's visionary approach to modern sacred spaces.

Address: Baumgartner Höhe 1, 1140 Vienna

Public transport: Bus 48A to Otto Wagner Spital

Hours: Sat-Sun 2 p.m. – 4 p.m.

Online: www.steinhofkirche.at

Postsparkasse | Postal Savings Bank

Historical Significance: The Postsparkasse is one of Otto Wagner's crowning achievements, embodying his ideals of modernity and functional beauty. Built using cutting-edge materials like aluminum and reinforced concrete, the building's minimalist design and light-filled interiors set a new standard for modern European architecture.

Address: Georg-Coch-Platz 2, 1010 Vienna

Public transport: U1, U3 to Stephansplatz

Hours: Mon-Fri 9 a.m. – 5 p.m.

Online: www.postsparkasse.at

Kaiserpavillon | Imperial Pavilion at Hietzing

Historical Significance: Originally designed as a private station for Emperor Franz Joseph, this pavilion reflects Otto Wagner's ability to merge imperial grandeur with modern design. The Kaiserpavillon is part of the Stadtbahn system and is a testament to Wagner's forward-thinking approach to public infrastructure and royal commissions.

Kaiserpavillon | Imperial Pavilion at Hietzing

Address: Schönbrunn Palace grounds, 1130 Vienna

Public transport: U4 to Hietzing

Hours: Check the website for guided tours

Online: www.wienmuseum.at

Wienzeilenhäuser | Residential Buildings on Linke Wienzeile

Historical Significance: These iconic apartment buildings on Linke Wienzeile, including the Majolikahaus, the building at Linke Wienzeile 38, and the building at Köstlergasse 3, exemplify Wagner's Art Nouveau style. The facades feature bold geometric patterns and colorful tiles, reflecting Wagner's belief that architecture should be functional and beautiful. These buildings remain among the most recognizable examples of his residential work in Vienna.

Address: Linke Wienzeile, 1060 Vienna

Public transport: U4 to Kettenbrückengasse

Hours: Exterior view only

Online: www.wien.info

Grave of Otto Wagner

Hietzing Cemetery: Group 13, Grave 113

Address: Maxingstraße 15, 1130 Vienna

Public transport: U4 to Hietzing

Hours: Daily, check website for seasonal times

Online: www.friedhoefewien.at

Viennese Modernism of Adolf Loos and Egon Schiele

At the turn of the 20th century, Vienna was a hotbed of cultural, artistic, and intellectual ferment. As the capital of the Austro-Hungarian Empire, the city was at the heart of a rapidly modernizing Europe, and it witnessed the birth of some of the most groundbreaking artistic movements in history. Among the most influential figures in this dynamic period were the architect and theorist

Adolf Loos and the expressionist painter Egon Schiele. Both men were central to the development of Viennese Modernism. Still, they approached the movement from radically different angles—Loos from the perspective of architecture and design and Schiele through painting and visual art.

Despite their medium differences, Loos and Schiele were united by a desire to break with tradition, reject the constraints of the past, and explore the deeper truths of human existence and modern life. Through their works, they challenged societal norms, embraced individual expression, and laid the groundwork for the future of modern art and architecture.

The Modernism of Adolf Loos

Adolf Loos (1870–1933) was one of the most influential architects and thinkers of his time, known for his stark rejection of ornamentation and his pioneering contributions to functionalist design. In contrast to the Art Nouveau movement, which was flourishing in Vienna during the early 20th century and was celebrated for its decorative, flowing forms, Loos advocated for a radical break from excessive decoration. His 1908 essay "Ornament and Crime" became a manifesto for modernist architecture, condemning the use of ornament as wasteful, backward, and a sign of degeneracy.

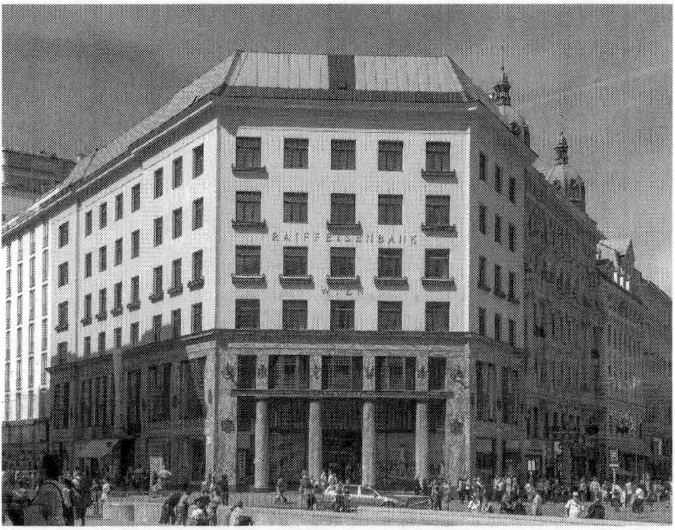

The Looshaus, Michaelerplatz

Loos argued that true modernity required simplicity, utility, and a focus on function. He believed that architecture and design should prioritize the needs of the individual and that excessive ornament was an unnecessary distraction. His disdain for ornamentation was not just aesthetic but also moral; he saw it as symptomatic of a society clinging to outdated traditions and failing to move forward into a rational, modern future. For Loos, the essence of modern architecture lay in the purity of form and the clarity of function.

One of the most famous examples of Loos' architectural philosophy is the Looshaus in Vienna, located on Michaelerplatz, near the Hofburg Palace. Completed in 1911, the building was a stark contrast to the surrounding neoclassical and baroque architecture. Its plain, unadorned facade—with smooth stone surfaces and clean, geometric lines—was met with shock and outrage by the Viennese public and critics alike. Many saw it as an affront to the city's imperial grandeur, and it was even dubbed "the house without eyebrows" due to its lack of decorative window moldings. Despite the initial controversy, the Looshaus is now recognized as a landmark of modernist architecture, embodying Loos' belief in simplicity and the elimination of superfluous ornamentation.

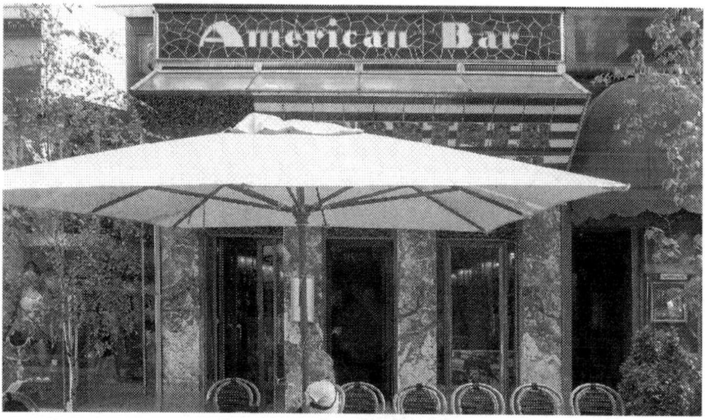

American Bar by Adolf Loos

Loos' influence extended beyond architecture to the realms of interior design and furniture. He designed spaces that were functional yet elegant, with a focus on high-quality materials like marble, wood, and leather. His interiors were notable for their restrained aesthetics, relying on the inherent beauty of the materials rather than elaborate decoration. One of his most famous interiors is the American Bar in Vienna, completed in 1908. This tiny space, designed with a rich palette of materials like onyx, dark wood, and mirrors, remains a masterpiece of minimalist elegance and a testament to Loos' genius for creating functional yet refined environments.

Loos' radical ideas about architecture and design were inextricably linked to his views on modern life. He believed that the role of the architect was not to impose a decorative vision but to create spaces that served the needs of contemporary people. In this sense, Loos was a forerunner of the functionalist movement that would later be championed by figures like Le Corbusier and the Bauhaus school. His influence on the development of modern architecture cannot be overstated, and his rejection of ornament in favor of function helped to define the aesthetic of the 20th century.

Egon Schiele and the Exploration of the Human Psyche

While Adolf Loos was reshaping the physical landscape of Vienna with his architectural innovations, Egon Schiele (1890–1918) was pushing the boundaries of visual art, creating deeply personal and often disturbing works that explored the complexities of the human condition. Schiele, a protégé of Gustav Klimt, was part of the Expressionist movement, which sought to express emotional experience rather than physical reality. His art was characterized by its raw intensity, psychological depth, and its unflinching exploration of themes like sexuality, death, and alienation.

Schiele's work was often seen as provocative and scandalous in his time. His stark, contorted figures—many of which were self-portraits—exposed the vulnerabilities, desires, and fears that lurk beneath the surface of the human psyche. Unlike Klimt, whose sensual portrayals of the female body were wrapped in layers of gold and intricate patterns, Schiele's nudes were stripped bare, both physically and emotionally. His figures often appear twisted or distorted, their elongated limbs and gaunt faces conveying a sense of anguish or existential turmoil.

Schiele's exploration of sexuality was particularly controversial. His drawings and paintings frequently featured nude models in explicit poses, which led to accusations of pornography and even resulted in his brief imprisonment in 1912 on charges of immorality. Despite—or perhaps because of—this controversy, Schiele's work captured the attention of avant-garde circles in Vienna and beyond. His art reflected a modernist preoccupation with the darker aspects of human nature and the subconscious, aligning him with the psychoanalytic theories of Sigmund Freud, another towering figure of Viennese modernism.

One of Schiele's most iconic works is "Self-Portrait with Raised Bare Shoulder" (1912), which exemplifies his unique approach to self-representation. In this painting, Schiele's gaunt figure is set against a stark, almost empty background, his intense gaze directed at the viewer. His body is twisted in a way that seems both vulnerable and confrontational, reflecting the tension between self-exposure and self-protection that is central to his work. This self-portrait, like many of Schiele's works, conveys a sense of psychological depth that goes beyond mere representation, offering a glimpse into the artist's inner world.

Schiele's focus on the darker, more unsettling aspects of life extended to his depictions of death and decay. His fascination with the fragility of the human body and the inevitability of death is evident in works like "Death and the Maiden" (1915), in which the themes of love and death are intertwined in a haunting embrace. The painting, created during World War I, reflects the anxieties of the time and the pervasive sense of loss and destruction that defined the era.

Tragically, Schiele's life was cut short in 1918 when he died of the Spanish flu at the age of 28, just days after his pregnant wife Edith. Despite his short career, Schiele produced a vast body of work that has had a lasting impact on the art world. His bold exploration of human sexuality, his psychological insight, and his willingness to confront taboo subjects marked him as one of the most important figures of Viennese Modernism. Today, Schiele's works are celebrated for their emotional intensity and their unflinching portrayal of the human experience, and they continue to resonate with contemporary audiences.

The Intersection of Architecture and Art in Viennese Modernism

Though Adolf Loos and Egon Schiele worked in different mediums, their contributions to Viennese Modernism were deeply interconnected, reflecting broader trends in the city's intellectual and cultural life. Both men were part of a wider movement that sought to break free from the constraints of tradition and explore new ways of seeing and experiencing the world. Their works, while radically different in form, shared a common rejection of ornamental excess and a commitment to expressing deeper truths about modern life.

In many ways, Loos and Schiele represented two sides of the same modernist coin: Loos with his emphasis on the rational, functional aspects of architecture and design, and Schiele with his exploration of the emotional, psychological dimensions of human existence. Both men were engaged in a dialogue with the past, challenging the old ways of thinking and creating space for new, more honest expressions of the modern condition.

Vienna, at the time, was a city undergoing significant transformation. It was a place where psychoanalysis, modernist art, architecture, and literature were flourishing, each field influencing the others in profound ways. Figures like Sigmund Freud, Gustav Klimt, and Karl Kraus were also part of this vibrant cultural landscape, and their ideas about the nature of the self, the role of art, and the function of society permeated the works of Loos, Schiele, and their contemporaries.

The Legacy of Loos and Schiele

Adolf Loos and Egon Schiele shaped Viennese Modernism, leaving a lasting impact on art, architecture, and modernist thought. Loos pioneered functionalist design, while Schiele's raw, expressive art delved into the human condition. Both challenged societal norms, pushing boundaries in their disciplines. Their innovative legacies continue to inspire and define modernism in Vienna and beyond.

Adolf Loos in Vienna

Looshaus | Adolf Loos' Landmark of Modernism

Historical Significance: The Looshaus, located on Michaelerplatz, is one of Adolf Loos' most famous works and a defining example of his rejection of ornamentation. Its simple, unadorned facade was a radical departure from the decorative historicism that dominated Vienna at the time. The building's minimalist design, with smooth stone surfaces and large windows, caused controversy when it was completed in 1911 but has since become a symbol of Viennese modernism.

Address: Michaelerplatz 3, 1010 Vienna

Public transport: U3 to Herrengasse

Hours: Exterior view only

American Bar | A Masterpiece of Interior Design

Historical Significance: The American Bar, also known as the Loos Bar, is a small yet iconic interior designed by Adolf Loos in 1908. Despite its limited size, Loos used luxurious materials like onyx, dark wood, and mirrors to create a sophisticated and intimate atmosphere. The bar reflects Loos' minimalist approach to design and his belief that beauty should come from materials and function rather than excessive decoration.

Address: Kärntner Durchgang 10, 1010 Vienna

Public transport: U1, U3 to Stephansplatz

Hours: Mon-Sun 12 p.m. – 4 a.m.

Online: www.loosbar.at

Knize | Modehaus Knize am Graben

Historical Significance: The Modehaus Knize, designed by Adolf Loos in 1910, is a menswear boutique that exemplifies his philosophy of functional elegance. The shop's interior is characterized by clean lines, high-quality materials, and a refined sense of luxury without the use of ornamentation. Loos' design for Knize has become a lasting example of modernist interior design in retail spaces.

Address: Graben 13, 1010 Vienna

Public transport: U1, U3 to Stephansplatz

Hours: Mon-Fri 10 a.m. – 6 p.m., Sat 10 a.m. – 5 p.m.

Online: www.knize.at

Leopold Museum | The Largest Schiele Collection

Historical Significance: The Leopold Museum houses the world's largest collection of Egon Schiele's works, including iconic self-portraits, landscapes, and nudes. As a leading figure in Viennese Expressionism, Schiele's intense and often provocative style is explored in depth here, showcasing his bold exploration of the human psyche.

Address: Museumsplatz 1, 1070 Vienna

Public transport: U2, U3 to Volkstheater

Hours: Daily 10 a.m. – 6 p.m.

Online: www.leopoldmuseum.org

Belvedere | Schiele's Expressionist Masterpieces

Historical Significance: The Belvedere holds a number of important works by Egon Schiele, including "Death and the Maiden," which reflects his fascination with mortality and the human condition. As part of its extensive Austrian art collection, the museum offers a glimpse into Schiele's unique contribution to Viennese Modernism.

Address: Prinz Eugen-Straße 27, 1030 Vienna

Public transport: Tram D to Schloss Belvedere

Hours: Daily 10 a.m. – 6 p.m.

Online: www.belvedere.at

Wien Museum | Adolf Loos' Architectural Legacy

Historical Significance: One of the highlights of the permanent exhibition at the Wien Museum Karlsplatz is the **living room with fireplace** from Adolf Loos' own apartment. This rare, authentically preserved interior offers a unique glimpse into Loos' design principles, showcasing his 1903 vision of functional beauty and simplicity. The room exemplifies his artistic approach to interior design, where he applied his principles of minimalist elegance and focus on material quality. Loos' influence on Vienna's architectural landscape is also explored through models and designs of his iconic buildings, including the Looshaus and American Bar.

Address: Karlsplatz, 1040 Vienna

Public transport: U1, U2, U4 to Karlsplatz

Hours: Tue-Sun 10 a.m. – 6 p.m.

Online: www.wienmuseum.at

Adolf Loos' Grave

Historical Significance: Karlsplatz is the living room with a fireplace from Adolf Loos' apartment. This rare, authentically preserved interior offers a unique glimpse into Loos' design principles, showcasing his 1903 vision of functional beauty and simplicity. The room exemplifies his artistic approach to interior design, where he applied his principles of minimalist elegance and focused on material quality.

Zentralfriedhof: Group 0, Row 1, Number 105

Address: Simmeringer Hauptstraße 234, 1110 Vienna

Public transport: Tram 71 to Zentralfriedhof, Tor 2

Hours: Daily, check website for seasonal times

Online: www.friedhoefewien.a

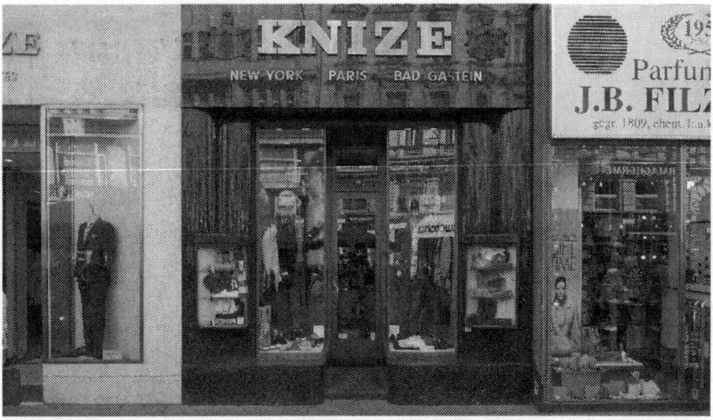

The Modehaus Knize

Egon Schiele in Vienna

Wien Museum | Exploring Schiele's Vienna

Historical Significance: The Wien Museum features works by Egon Schiele and places him within the broader context of Vienna's artistic and cultural development during the early 20th century. Exhibitions here highlight the intense psychological depth and raw emotion in Schiele's art.

Address: Karlsplatz, 1040 Vienna

Public transport: U1, U2, U4 to Karlsplatz

Hours: Tue-Sun 10 a.m. – 6 p.m.

Online: www.wienmuseum.at

Albertina | Schiele's Drawings and Watercolors

Historical Significance: The Albertina holds a significant collection of Schiele's drawings and watercolor. His expressive line work and bold compositions can be viewed alongside works by his contemporaries, providing deeper insight into his influence on modern art.

Address: Albertinaplatz 1, 1010 Vienna

Public transport: U1, U2, U4 to Karlsplatz

Hours: Daily 10 a.m. – 6 p.m.

Online: www.albertina.at

Hietzinger Hauptstraße 114 | Schiele's Place of Death

Historical Significance: Egon Schiele tragically died here at the age of 28 during the 1918 Spanish flu pandemic, just three days after his pregnant wife Edith passed. This house marks the site where the short but intense life of one of Austria's greatest artists came to an end.

Address: Hietzinger Hauptstraße 114, 1130 Vienna

Public transport: U4 to Hietzing

Hours: Exterior view only

Schiele's Grave

Historical Significance: Egon Schiele is buried in the Ober St. Veit Cemetery (Group B, Row 10, Number 15), where visitors can pay their respects to the artist whose life and work left an indelible mark on Viennese Modernism. His modest grave contrasts with the powerful impact his art continues to have.

Address: Gemeindeberggasse 26, 1130 Vienna

Public transport: U4 to Ober St. Veit

Hours: Daily, check website for seasonal times

Online: www.friedhoefewien.at/friedhof-ober-st.-veit

Printed in Poland
by Amazon Fulfillment
Poland Sp. z o.o., Wrocław

55687803R00085